Darkness Inside Out

RODNEY PYBUS was born in Newcastle upon Tyne in 1938 and educated at Rossall School and Gonville & Caius College, Cambridge, where he read Classics and English. In the 1960s and 1970s he worked in the north-east of England as a newspaper journalist and a writer-producer in television, specialising in documentary films, and arts and education programmes. He was a Lecturer in Mass Communication in the School of English & Linguistics at Macquarie University, Sydney, 1976–79.

After working for Northern Arts in Cumbria and the Lake District, he moved in 1983 to Suffolk, where he still lives. He has taught creative writing at all levels of education from primary schools to universities and adult education, and English Literature and Media Studies to A level students.

He was for many years a co-editor of the literary quarterly *Stand* (founded by the poet Jon Silkin in 1952), and has given readings of his poetry widely in Britain, and also in Ireland, France, South Africa, Australia and the Canary Isles. His writing has appeared in the United States, Australia, Russia, Denmark, Spain and France, and been translated into French, Spanish, Russian, Czech, German and Romanian.

Awards and prizes include a Hawthornden Fellowship; Arts Council of Great Britain Writer's Fellowships in Suffolk and Cambridge; The Poetry Society's Alice Hunt Bartlett Prize; Society of Authors travel grant; first prize, Peterloo International Poetry Competition; major prizes in the National Poetry Competition and the Arvon International Poetry Competition.

Also by Rodney Pybus from Carcanet Press

Cicadas in Their Summers: New & Selected Poems

Flying Blues

RODNEY PYBUS

Darkness Inside Out

Northern House

CARCANET

First published in Great Britain in 2012 by
Northern House
In association with Carcanet Press Limited
Alliance House
Cross Street
Manchester M2 7AQ

www.carcanet.co.uk

A CIP catalogue record for this book is available from the British Library

ISBN 978 1 84777 201 5

The publisher acknowledges financial assistance from Arts Council England

Supported by
ARTS COUNCIL
ENGLAND

Typeset by XL Publishing Services, Tiverton
Printed and bound in England by SRP Ltd, Exeter

for Ella
as ever
Lawrence & Richard

Acknowledgements

Some of these poems were first published in *Jacket* (online), *London Magazine*, *Notre Dame Review* (USA), *Poetry Ireland Review*, *PN Review*, *Poetry Review*, *Salt Magazine* (online), *Stand*, *Victorian Studies Journal* (USA), *Wallace Stevens Journal* (USA)

'Moycullen' appeared in *The Cúirt Journal* 2 (ed. Trish Fitzpatrick; Galway Arts Centre, 1994)

'Flesh Markets' appeared in *An Idea of Bosnia* (ed. David H.W. Grubb; Autumn House/Feed the Children, 1996)

'Quartet for the Lion' was included in *Comparative Criticism* 19: 'Literary Devolution: Writing in Scotland, Ireland, Wales and England' (ed. E.S. Shaffer; Cambridge UP, 1997)

'October Flowers in Prague' appeared in *Beyond Lament* (ed. Marguerite Striar; Northwestern UP, USA, 1998)

'Speaking of Angels' was published in *Light Unlocked: Christmas Card Poems* (eds. Kevin Crossley-Holland & Lawrence Sail; Enitharmon, 2005)

'Reading the Air at Southwold', as 'Taking the Air at Southwold', won a major prize in the Arvon International Poetry Competition and was published in the 2006 *Arvon International Poetry Competition Anthology*

'Darkness Inside Out' is due to appear in *The Laurel Crown: An Anthology of Poems and Portraits* (edited and photographed by Jemimah Kuhfeld; forthcoming)

Grateful thanks to the Society of Authors for the assistance of a grant to aid research and travel in South Africa.

Contents

Leaves from Each Tree

Down on the Cape

Back to the Future

Still a Way from Good Hope

Leaves from Each Tree

Veronica Lake

The earth was small, light blue and so touchingly alone... our home that must be defended like a holy relic.

Aleksei Leonov (Russian cosmonaut)

They'll take your ashes if you have the cash,
Capsuled and hammocked somewhere between death
And immortality... for a few years only.
Some trip, precious! – nearly five thousand dollars
For a teaspoonful to be swept up at five miles a second

Aboard the latest shiny, shiny *Pegasus*.
This is a very dear suspension of dust and
Disbelief: just seven grammes of your old self
Circling our poor relic marble every ninety minutes.
This pinch of powder, this *soupçon* of you-ness,

Like the desiccated scurf of the original spurt
That started your smidgen of history ticking,
Will have to come back down again,
Flaring and smoking, all the way down again.
You can't cheat the snap of oblivion's jaws.

Littering space with gizmos and garbage
Has no more hope than trying to write names
On stone or bronze or water.
Cruising the whirled beauty of our planet's
All very well, but what's the point if you can't *see*

The brown foot of Arabia or the speedwell
Blue of the seas? The cloud-swirls like
Uncooked pavlova draped from Cape to Cape?
What's the point if there's no fun or feeling? No wonder?
The corporate deals of *Celestial Burial Services*

Playing half-speed Puck with my bone-dust
And brain-ash are no miracle – what I'd want's to see
From up there the million places one life's too brief for,
To play my own games with time and space,
Like wondering if that little town by the coast

Of Argentina, down there, across the Plate
From Montevideo, might have a brightening pool
Of inland water near... I'd like to mix up maps and names
And multiply the shades of Veronica Lake
(And a fresh *Blue Dahlia*?), then I'd zoom out like

A satellite camera or, better still, like
The imagination, and try to find her face below,
Emblazoned on a handkerchief of cloud
Stretching to the Andes, framing her there...
And she's staring up at me, Constance, peekaboo.

Borderline

These varieties of ignorance, like the levels
of the manifold earth, pose more questions than you
or I could shake a stick at – the man from Mull

buried at Bamburgh after the Romans left,
vowel changes in Caucasian dialects or the incidence
of spoonbills in eastern England… and to think

that till yesterday I knew nothing or little
of the provinces of Euskara, three in France,
four in Spain, a hybrid region of allegation

and discontent, with all the houses spruced up
in the same colours in village after village,
snow-white, dark forest, and drying blood.

We've heard the claim of Basque to be older than
all our European tongues and no relation,
but I knew nothing of its sounding like rapid fire,

the Rs and Ks and Xs doubling up, clattering, whooshing,
crackling like old maxims, and I didn't know how green
were the foothills of their western Pyrenees inland

south-east from Baiona, rising forests of pine
and surprising oak, mists wafting through
like pulled gauze over concealed valleys

and inscrutable paths that led, seemingly,
from one country to another – which is an insult
as deep as soil or syntax to those who belong

to these Basque lands. And I did not know that,
over these rich fields and stone outcrops
that could easily have been another border long ago troubled

by blood and reivers, I could expect to see vultures
circling unconcerned by this side or that
of a borderline unmarked by tree or stone or water.

Quartet for the Lion

i.m. Leos Janáček 1854–1928

Even the greatest beauty of tone feels cold if the artist
has not the strength to break it – or if not to break it, to
boil over – even if not dying, to burn – even if not to
burn, to hurry – even if not to hurry, to exaggerate.

'The sea, the earth', Hukvaldy, 10 June 1926
(trans. Vilem & Margaret Tausky)

(i) *Leaves from each tree*

Art's no soft touch. They are the disciplines
of his own fire, these days
he thrashes the ivories
till the brightness stops him,
finger-ends dripping as if
above the mouth of a broken fighter.

Yet how he can make silence fall too:
the leaves from each tree
to the ground.

Everything he knows has a voice, and through
such windows as tone makes clear
he plays an inspector of souls:
not just the women snatched from gossip on a tram
but the robin on the fence-post,
the cry of a vixen disappearing
into the wood, one of his hens saying goodnight
from the garden table.

He cups his smiling hands
round every drop of sound: makes light of contradictions
as, after all, fluid with possibility.
Every breaking of silence he counts

as a lovely shock to his ear, brief patterns of fissure
he will make inventions from,
and down whatever discordant path

his notes give voice back to the world,
he finds phrases so intimate sometimes
in their soft hammering that they can
draw out, then shake loose a poised
insistent tear.
And his tunes cut like wire.

(ii) *Olga and the others*

Just a few notes at a time,
she never spoke for long.

His daughter's voice, even in her teens,
always took the composer by surprise.
Her low voice, shy.
But memory scribbled enough
for an *adagio* later
for Olga, the fresh flowers on her grave,

and an overgrown path
in the woods near Hukvaldy.

Those pale notes now
are like seeds from the grass brought down
by the passing blade,

and seeding, year over year,
their lovely selves.

(iii) *Not symphoniously, but the* Kreutzer

There are none so deaf...
as those blinded by the flashbulbs.
Out of sight and earshot
he waits, not biding his years, teaching
not for a talent's *faute de mieux*
pupils with straw in their heads.
The confident hair of his youth goes white.

Some filch their sounds
from where they're told heaven lies,
their fame levitating
on the puffs of the crowd's applause,
crying *Holy, holy, holy*
our marvellously abstract art!

He makes the swirling world
his own, not so much in the dancing place
of instruments, not symphoniously,

but with the voice, the raw song
and a human hand scrubbing, impassioned,
at a string.

He makes of love an off-beat, a guttural sentence
in a dialect as gentle as butter, and a snatch
of bird-call hard to bear.

At dusk he sits under the rustle
of the trees' approval. And even this
he could annotate,
looking into the world, tuning it,
remembering how it begins: *'It is early spring*
and the second day of our journey...'

(iv) *Madam, the source*

Is it a path or a stream? I love these lime trees,
the flowers blown and falling

that will need sweeping, and the leaves, later.
We can sit for hours, too easily, surrounded by good ideas

going brown. Is it a path or a stream?
Madam, when in 1917 I saw your tears,

your child in your arms, your husband away
to war... It must always come from life, he said,

refusing a ride back home on the tram, all its Brno names
rattling away in German.

The notes don't just sit down on the keys!
Madam, these letters of mine, these small black notes…

Tunes that hit like water. I too need a town with a river
through it like a throat, and the voices rushing,

sawing back and forth, bows on the strings. Intimate life.
He was right, the old *maestro*, ready to climb the path

up through the forest, to put his palm to the trickle
where the river starts: it is so slight but gathering,

like a child pulling a wooden cart over cobbles,
like the song of the goldfinch which breaks every day

through the bars of her owner's cage, like your voice
through its tears, the shout in the street

before the bullets and the bloody fighting.
It all begins in life: he showed me

how a cadence of love, of pain, speaks and dies;
how strongly its memory rivers into song.

Speaking of Angels

I don't believe in angels
(even when I can see them lined up more than fifty feet

above my head
back to back in pairs as if uncertain about what's to be or not)

I'm quite impervious
to the pale curtains they wear for dresses, their gold-plate

haloes and curls
and bedtime-story wings like quattrocento Disney

supposed to make you
trust the status of their prequels and special announcements

The ones above me now
I can see by the clerestory's falling light were once spangled

in red and green and silver –
so high up they escaped Cromwell's lads on the rampage in 1644

and I will admit to
their faded wooden charms… but the kind of inspired uttering

I can take more happily
on trust comes from the crafty player of a baryton

that's like a rare enhanced viol
a cello look-alike with secret strings whose plucked notes as well as bowed

tell me something
more persuasive, not to say heavenly, from their steel and gut –

that what's most sublime
is what's most human, soaring right up to the startled angels

and beyond,
their wings outstretched like transfixed fliers

(say, silver-streaked
hawk moths or some other casual migrants)

as if unable to resist
this awkward truth, but still gaping in disbelief

(at Blythburgh Church, Suffolk)

Cob and Pen

for Ken Smith and Judi Benson, May 2003

The pen is back after
An absence of days.
Brooding, shuffling, settling…
We should be so lucky.
You know the feeling
And so do I, though they,
Cob and pen, know what
Will come, as we do not
Who write stuff, I tell myself,
Walking the dogs past
Each day her island nest,
Reed-throne like a green
And tidy platter. More words
That once someone like me
Would have cut a quill
From one like her, to make sense of.

(Even now, on the screen, I can
Tap out into visibility
'Quill' and 'pen' as if
To conjure a flight-feather,
Trimmed and pertinent with ink,
That might scratch 'Havana
And back', or in your case
'Hell and back' – you
With your grand pen.)

The cob stands up high
In fast-running water
And flaps his great sheets
At me, with a hissing loud
Enough to put frighteners
On a bull-terrier called Poppy.
Brave cob, look after her,
This year, next year, and on –

Your precious pen, and neither
Properly mute, nor will be.

So, without any of the old bird/
Word games, back to work
In almost too-green meadows
Where this early-summer morning
I'd like to fetch you (still penned in,
Still indoors, isolated
With the light behind you) some
Canny ideas that come in drifts
Like earthy constellations
Of buttercups… and above,
Swifts wheel and hurtle past,
Black minute-birds that stop
For none of us. But for
Your return, your re-entry into
The no longer trite 'land of the living'
I wish you both, pen and cob,
A song-thrush on the shed roof,
All spotty with tune.

i.m. Ken Smith (1938–2003)

Small Illuminations

i.m. Françoise Trichet 1945–2011

The unturning sun-flowers invisible, vineyards *plus noir*
than a dark red from Cahors… it's wearing pretty thin, this high old

black-out stuff, as if the stars were light coming through
its threadbare weave, and beyond it another high bleaching sun

might be throbbing over Spain, and black specks of buzzard
remotely cruising towards noon, calling to each other

strangely like motherless kittens. It's late
but still too early for the aerolites' big display

when they'll shoot like pyre sparks or prayers, sprightly
on their way to nothing. Friends for more than half our lives

the three of us peer upwards into the space that says we
are little or nothing: I think to myself we shouldn't keep on

turning them into hope or fame, or fates to steer our lives by.
They've carried too much for us, our heavens

and their tremendous tales. That dropping point of light to the west –
was that a falling moment of disappointment years ago,

not quite forgotten, one second out of all our mutual hours?
In the slippery grass the day's long scent congeals

where cicadas go on and on like unanswered phones. They are callers
of desperate patience. An owl clatters onto the barn roof.

And off again, something puling from its claws.
In Gascony now three middle-aging accidentals, pausing briefly,

should know better that epiphanies must bring more
than sighs or gawping of an August night.

Growing cold, we do not wait the hours
till the Perseids' 3 a.m. finale. There's no pattern up there

we shall see. Yet already near the house, in the long grass
I'd meant to trim, there's a pair of beetle-stars before us,

with their blue-green glow like a locked-in passion melting
into light, and another by the threshold of *Le Soulan*.

These three lined up on a page would hardly be enough
to learn a lyric by, and I tell myself to read nothing

into the illumination shed by these wingless unfalling
female stars that cling to earth. They squeeze themselves

up tight and play dead. I don't think they know
how shining they are in this tangled blackness.

(at Beaucaire-sur-Baïse)

Chanteloube *and the Pleasures of the Text*

for Brian and Jan Ambler

What a shifty text, what a maze, the inscriptions of light
and bird and flower… and how we keep licking our dry lips
and trying to peer beyond the bottom of the page!

Yet at each whirling circle the invisible strings
tighten the swallows about me in twos and threes,
and you, returning from the cool house,

cannot cut them free, so in this garden, already
after noon, I feel suspiciously like the hungry man
at a tyrant's feast, afraid to gorge

on the gorgeous food that might do for him:
young red-faced finches chatter in the wistaria,
bees are drowning out the lavenders,

and, calling in at this flower and that, the pied admirals
tack across the property with more energy than the swallowtails
for all their creamy waltzing through the Charente.

Beyond the baked flower-beds, and tomatoes swollen
with vermilion, the young vines are doing something
with the sunshine I hope to appreciate while

there's still time enough. The door into the little *chai*
in the old barn is ajar: darkness delays pleasure
(no, don't rush!), and, for now, the great lump of heat

presses down on this tail-end of July.
'Maiden again!' was a classroom joke, if you remember,
but that way of saying it's caught in cobwebs now.

Should we mind the Greeks with their pithy *mots*
about *'nothing too much'*, and their watery wine?
Such fruits they found on the road to excess,

and looked back in panic from the other side
of some median jouissance. *'Keep out – Gods only!'*
From here I may meet them coming back.

Now I can reveal, as they say, that I am dreaming,
here in slack inducements of shade under a catalpa tree,
of the possibilities of tomorrow's grand salamander,

its speckled cool that fire isn't supposed to touch.
Let's invent it now, lurking in the cistern, circling briskly
and unfazed in the water. It will be there – it *will* be! –

though we shall not know what to do with it,
nor how to talk to it, with its cold eyes and impossible age…
another crumpled leaf comes rustling down past me,

like one more of these dog-days' unanswered letters.
Almost unnoticed, a black bug eases between
the pale-pinkish, oddly sapid petals of her grace

the *Duchesse d'Angoulême*, provoking anxiety
(remember what happened to the rose in the howling storm)
in the anthologist's imagination.

Without wishing to, I glance up again
at the canopy of leaves and the ten-inch pods
of scabbardy brown wittily poised above my face.

(From here I can't determine whether
l'Abbé Bignon in the king's library ever saw *in situ*
the trumpets of the new world *Kutuhlpa*

or not, but the tree is palpably here.
What a privilege – *bignoniaceous*! Not, of course,
that I'm crazy about such nominations. Not much.)

The fracture, the sheer smash of it
when it comes, long after the fissures across the dark sky
to the south-west, is harder to take because invisible,

ungraspable – a lambeg-booming roll uncoiling,
portentous in its pauses and percussions melding
and dying on one note. *(Why is that noise, Daddy?)*

We are, alas, de-signers all, nothing will redeem us.
But what does it mean here, 'alas'? The thunder's still
bashing and cracking away out over Biscay

(think of the strings in *Katya*'s third act), but the flowers,
the songs, are still bright here in the garden,
so imagine, in the curving shadow

of the cistern's little parapet, Bacchus,
old and tabby, is for once caught napping.
Imagine again, *au jour le jour*!

Mariana Now

for David & Dawn Latané

> *She only said, 'My life is dreary.*
> *He cometh not,' she said;*
> *She said, 'I am aweary, aweary,*
> *I would that I were dead!'*

Tennyson, 'Mariana'

Much of the night she sat by the open window,
  Six floors up, watching garbage blow like leaves
Down orange streets. After midnight traffic had thinned,
  Yet cars still screamed away from the lights
On Poplar Street, where no green leaf, she imagined,
  But gutter-grass had grown for a hundred years.

Salmon-pink geraniums were dead-dry in their pots;
  Rusty petals fell to the window-sill whenever
They caught her eye. Nothing when she flicked the channels
  But garden make-overs and cookery gross-outs.
She knew she'd get no chance on *Dating Game*. Didn't want it.
  While she stared into space, the walls moved in.

No tunes. No text. Even with her shiny mobile phone
  She hadn't left the flat – she knew it was superstition,
Like not stepping on pavement lines for fear of shocks.
  She trapped the bathroom bluebottle in a jar
And for an hour or so watched it go mad in fits
  And starts. She paced her cell, from sigh to sigh.

Why wouldn't he...? She cut out pages from *Hello!*
  And pinned them everywhere, all the famous smiles
To smile at her. She wished she had a clock that ticked and struck
  Each hour of her life, that would make her a mark on silence.
She lay on the bed and got up again, head full of white noise
  Like static pain. Outside, she heard loud boys and a girl.

She dozed in the only chair and re-lived yesterday
    And the day before, missed the start of the spattering drops,
The rising wind that picked through the *News of the World*.
    She stared out over bracelets of city lights, listening
To a CD by Dark Side of the Moon with Ms Ultra Brite.
    It began to dawn she was too old for this, five years at least.

The filmy nets were swirling back into the room.
    She yearned for those venetians you get in classy *noirs*
Or some heavy red velvet stuff. But not for this dump.
    The windows in the block of flats across the street,
Little rectangles of '90s misery, were dark by 2 a.m.
    Nothing framed and lit like movie-shots, of lives with verve or fun

Or passion. She lay down again, shut her eyes, and tried to count
    How many pills would make a metre… she was too hot
And too cold, she was too bored, too young, too old.
    The sky was paling, like an effort of light through a grey sheet.
She threw the silver phone across the room and hoped
    With all her empty heart no sun would shine.

'Oh what's the point? – he'll never call,'
    She said to herself, aloud, again.
She was so tired of tears and pain.
        Over and over, 'No point at all.'

Cultural

It must be that
there are fewer cats these days
wheeling their low haunches
along the margins of small back gardens

where the honeysuckle pervades
and the roses are blowing
their pink and apricot petals
in the wind –

I'm not making this up, you know!
Some of the English
haven't yet surrendered to cheap decking
and cheeky coloured balls on sticks

imported from Ireland –
the garden birds are so tame
this year I can almost
scoop up a handful

of song-thrush
which not ten minutes ago
was smashing his way
into another helping of *escargots*.

And the jackdaws!
They've come slumming down
our end of Plough Lane,
leaving the posh chimney-pots

of Pevsner-land.
It's bloody difficult to read sometimes, outside
under the parasol, with all
the racket of their *badinage*

worse than traffic.
I had my head deep in *Cloud Atlas*
the other afternoon, or it might
have been Longley's *Snow Water*

for its quench and grace, when a common
or garden house sparrow,
exiting the hollyhock
behind me, clipped my neck

with the awkward tissue of his wing-tip.
I thought he'd flown till
I saw him on the ground
a yard away, the buff wings

of an ermine moth
as big as his own head
sticking out from his bill,
thrashing to its finale.

Up in the lime-tree
the collared doves
invisibly, from their vantage
pooh-poohed everything.

Three Hoopoes in a Drawer

for Tony Rudolf

I promise – no sliding panels, no mirrors! Come on – have a good look!
I open the top drawer and (under the retired mauve socks
marked '*Will Power*' from Stratford-on-Avon) reveal two inches
of smoked vermilion sealing-wax, a scrawled Fifties postcard from Soho,
reading **Big Chest for Sale**, half a wing off a tortoiseshell, and then

making a forced march with no compass into the hinterland, I come up with
a whole farmyard – somewhere near Aspatria under a muddy, long-suffering
afternoon sky, waiting for the late Sheila Fell and her palette of umber
                                                                    and slate.
Too early, wrong farm. Next, a pizza scoffed outside *The Golden Dragon*
                                                        in 1977.
That would have been Palm Beach. I mean, the one in New South Wales.
Blue water by Hockney. And now the air is fluttering by my left ear
from the deckle-edged vowels of a lovely Wienerin of a certain age:
we are dancing, cheekily, at her house in Gloriettegasse… and we are
                                                                    speaking
of her moody daughter and her daggering, that is to say, poignant, black looks
because I'm hugging, plushly, her *soignée* and sufficient mother – Frau Siedek
likes this, she tells me, warmly… but before anything more educational
                                                                    can occur

I find myself with a lucid arrangement of marble, a sea like aubergine,
and a ripe persimmon sun on its slow way down from heaven
over Apollo's temple at Sounion – I'd better see if it's still there,
the wretched John Smith's autograph, incised in 1810. Touch and go. *Touch
and go!* That's the rule. Suddenly there are Greek connections
whizzing everywhere, particles and pronouns from the past, whatevers
that shake you dizzy with discovery, like the hoopoe king I came across
                                                                    in my teens
in a comedy by someone even funnier than God. Since then

I've had this craving for a glimpse of your *echt* hoopoe, an exotic
in pancake make-up with excitable crest, and a couple of old-fashioned
Newcastle United wings. No luck for half a life-time… It's true, *Tereu*!

But now, this late summer day, I've opened the drawer – *et voilà*: three
hoopoes
feeding in a French paddock, decurving bills picking over the earth
like proofreaders who've lost their specs, still busy with the syntax of grass…
The pleasure comes with a rush and a grin, with a call of *hoo-poo-poo*
and the magpie kit, and who would not then put their hands together
for the shade of the great *maestro* Aristophanes?

Good that they take no notice of the brat on his coughing two-stroke
or the old dobbin plodging and squelching the field to clarts, or me, staring –
I stare till my eyes begin to dribble from deep inside with the delighted pain
that pirouettes round such a moment – so many times, past recollection,
I have found this drawer empty, all the birds flown without so much
as testing the air with fresh musics, the landscape bitter and sere,
as we used to say. And now? Trust me, they're here, I tell you, they're here.
Don't go and startle them with your disbelief –

The Man From Elsewhere

i.m. J.G. Farrell 1935–1979

for Derek Mahon

> ... *I had that sense*
> *of someone not quite there, yet not quite*
> *missing, as the small boat laboured on,*
>
> *someone who should have embarked on the other side,*
> *standing alone somewhere, on an empty quay*
> *that nothing could inhabit but desire.*

John Burnside, 'The Day Star'

Let enough years pass and the memories by themselves
begin to gather, swooping and chattering like birds,
and it's hell to hold them still or speak of their bright
particulars, as if the words that might measure out
a little understanding from the swirling *son et lumière*
are themselves eager only for fresh peregrinations.

I wanted to believe I'd see him again, a few nights after
I had been to 'Gortfahane', curious to see where
he'd settled in '79 and found his little plot of arcadia –
such a brief spell before that wave cuffed him from his fishing rock,
an outrider, perhaps, of the tempest still far out at sea.
I'd driven westwards from Tooreen on Sheehy Mountain,

and found it on the way to another Tooreen,
out beyond Bantry, an old stone farm-house
by Letter Mountain. I am not, God knows, in search
of lost hours, or tides missed ten thousand days ago:
I can hardly bear to admit, even to my daily self,
that it's fifty years or so since the last time,

when he was a fiery three-quarter in the red and white
hoops of our school's 1st XV rugby zephyr,
who went through tackles as if they were weeds;
he was one of the lordlings in those days,
one who had a seat at high table in the great hall.
Three years younger, I was just one more pebble

in the gravel wasteland of the quad, someone to
kick off the forbidden lawn of the Sumner Library
on his way to chapel. He was extraordinary even then,
with his pale colouring and blue eyes,
and the black hair already starting to silver – no,
the photos tell me, mysteriously, I've got that wrong.

I could no more in those days have talked to him
about Yeats's 'Byzantium' or *The Catcher in the Rye*
than I could have chatted to the shade of Achilles.
It is such a bizarre country, the 1950s, with its maps
encrypted in a long-lost decade, where you can just about
hang on to the slippery face of recollection,

where the sons of the well-heeled shivered and trembled
or pranced through their terms of privilege.
I often used to think, composing *faux-Tristia* for Latin prep,
that Ovid didn't have it so bad in his Black Sea exile.
JGF had it right, though – take what you want,
don't let it touch you, get out fast. Except – *odi*

et amo – when it's in your marrow you can't burn it out.
Long afterwards I picked up some footnotes:
that canny *Whisky Joe* had kept on recycling the same dictations –
'*point-virgule,*' he'd rasp in crispy Edinburgh French;
that the Head's wife, Dorothy Young, with a prow
like the *Ark Royal*, had lent us each the same novels

about Elizabeth I; that the *Nobby* Ilett I'd argued with
over Picasso and Bartok's quartets, who'd drilled rugby moves
into young Farrell, had once been Keith Douglas' closest friend;
that we had shared not only the same admixture of shyness
to arrogance, but also dreams of drowning;
that each of us, with *Mens Agitat Molem* running through

our centres, had left our *alma mater*, despite her veins of sleet,
with something rubbed into smouldering that might become
a writer's hard flame. And who were the great ones
who had gone before? Patrick Campbell and Leslie Charteris…
It would have been no great surprise to catch sight of him again,
in that lane that runs from 'Saltwater House'

(his name for it which never got to replace 'Gortfahane')
down to the gap-toothed jawline of Bantry Bay.
I have seen the apple and pear trees he planted,
I have thought of him tending courgettes and scallions,
preparing a hefty fresh-caught pollock of an evening,
picking sorrel by the back-door…

He walks past me, hands in pockets,
shoulders hunched against the edge of the wind off the Atlantic,
gives me a quick, quizzical look, half-smiling,
half-recognising, as if to say, 'What *do* you
think you're up to?' 'That's a good question, Jim,'
I call after him, but he has gone and I am waking already…

Why now, after so many decades?
The longest memories are often the brightest
(however murky their provenance), and reading his life,
revisiting the novels, has set them flying again.
Chance, for want of a better word, brought me to
that craggy green finger he'd chosen as his retreat

from London's fester and muddle – the usual things:
too little money, too much personal traffic at all hours –
and chance brought me to a meeting with
the genial tractor-driver who'd been his friend
and taught him to fish, who pointed out to me
'Gortfahane' half-hidden in the trees across the field.

And why *not* now? I can't accept they have the last words,
the gods, the fates, whatever if anything controls the intersections
in our lives, those crossing-points when we find ourselves
on the lip of infinity, and the lines are suddenly meeting
and not moving on. What dreadful line was it that joined
his Oxford iron lung to the grey choking in Bantry Bay?

Nothing at all, I suppose, nothing malicious,
greedy, revengeful, soul-battering. Nothing of intention.
No, I'm not sure, to answer his question, except
that when it's late in the day the next hour
always seems to have departed ahead of time.
I know for certain he's provoked a long list of wishes –

that we had met, not just as schoolboys, but as men,
perhaps in middle age when three years are only a wee pause
before re-winding the clock; that I could have joined the queue
to tell him that in our generation there wasn't a finer composer
of the music that fiction makes from what's been and gone;
that we could have swapped a few books and

stories of satirical pantos and the birth of politics,
of my Lady Macbeth (with Mrs Peters' sexy bra
padded 'top-full of direst cruelty'), of *Harry* and *Pansy*,
The Bin, and *Doggy* and the rest who straitened our lives
on that bleak outpost of the C. of E., stranded half-
way between Fleetwood fish docks and Blackpool Tower;

that the sea could have spared him to explore
other old maps that showed off in their raw-flesh pink
the sprawling atrocities of *imperium* and greed –
Jim Farrell v. Cecil Rhodes: what a match we missed!
That I might have introduced him to the rare
Lacrima di Morro d'Alba with its aftertaste of violets,

and that we'd raised a glass or three to
those of us who are always partly elsewhere
even when we're here in plain view.
Mid-August, and home from western Cork
I saw that all the swifts and most of the swallows
had already set off south for an African summer.

Too early this year, I thought. *Too early.*
Days later I was in the garden, snatching at
meagre hand-outs of sunshine on a wind-smashed day
when the cumulus was being torn apart
into grey piles of fluff and the finest spindrift –
to the west there was nothing

but the pale dullness of possible rain, what he liked
to call *lumière blafarde* – then right overhead came
a handful of martins wind-whirled and hurtling
almost out of control, and among them a dark flash
before it was out of sight behind the limes,
the clean sabre of a singular swift.

Bridling at Birdsong

It begins with a low draught that unfurls
                                        into wind, a white
            whirled through sound.
Can dogs do imagination as well? Are their pictures to ride?
The little disc spins brilliant sounds from its box,
and the walls take wing and water
                                        pours down from the books.
She has moved from the fireside to a point midway

between the finches' chirrup-cluster and the echo-mixture
                    twittering to the left,
                                        and the melt-stream's
                                        gargling spate to the right
            which began with single drops of water plinking
            from a height
                                into a cistern
                                        in the middle of the room.
                                        The air grows
black and visual with crows,
their coarse shouting like pages of distorting typeface
translated into air,
                        or rowdy wireless backbenchers
                        fighting for space
                        coarse in their dark suits.

Her ear-flaps go up and down, unhooked by distress;
the coal-smudged face, the blacker eyes, the brow in grooves
                                        of absorption tip-tilt
                    from side to side through the long first movement.
There are no words among these sounds, but I know
the north when I hear it, and I can tell you
                                        she's on the edge of

            something, a crevasse of puzzle,
as if there were a secret in there –
                                        why these sounds
have no scents of any kind.

No bird, no water, no tree, no cold.
Or so I read her. Can she do the imagination as well?
                              What is her intelligence of?

The fire purrs, the windows rattle, the strange
nor'easter rushes down the lane,
        geese are calling to each other as they pass
                        overhead across the ceiling
                              of suggested sky, bawling
their cold honking cries from straight throats
                              constrained by corners,
                and now wings are thrashing
lagoon-waters, fading into gull-screams fading into
                              surf-roaring

                and she's beginning to whine quietly
to herself. Or to me. Is it fear tugging?
Water-call? Snow-beckon?
                I feel it, the pull
of the whole orchestra,
                the dancing-place of the far north, behind closed eyes.
In each channel wings and screeching
grow louder, but she cannot know – can she? – this is composed
harshness,
                engineered to move us, blended, tweaked, re-
recorded into symphony, these birds in stereo from Sapmi.
                              I can't separate
                              without seeing
gull from gannet or tern from petrel but I can see
even without shutting my eyes the million million feather flakes
whirling against the black cliffs, salt cried over coal –

                does she see anything, intrepid, shaking,
beyond bookshelves, chair, computer-screen, speakers?
                Can she do, without language,

the transformations? She slinks, tail held low, beside my knee
and rolls up the big beads of her eyes towards me. The trouble is,
I can read anything I like in her steady gaze.
                              Swans beat up and down.

Rollers hammer the north. February outside,
and the arctic swells to fill my room. *Con anima cantabile*,
this long movement. Come on, little red dog –

                              sing these birds with me

as the Laplanders pass among us, the gas-fire lost in the sound
of their rattling bells and billowing horns.

                              They sing in a foreign language

and images rise from what I've never seen, the rolling
                              refrains weaving in
and out of the rattling wind
                    are rhythms of work or walking.
Swans come scudding in, clouding the sky. Maybe that's all
I need to know.
          Bells like wind-chimes, the grunting of heavy animals.
And the frog croaks from the pond, and my dog stares
and stares at me as if I had done all this for no good
                              reason she can tell of,

as if I had created these echoes of bird and water
that hang before us for a few seconds, and the gale
                              raising itself up
          on loud wings.

                    Reindeer crunch across the snow-carpet
                        and an hour has passed through us

and I can see that she hears the pictures, but not if she sees.
And what is it you see now, tracking these signs across
                              the white spaces,
this poetry of a red dog and my brown study,
                              without any
of the notes from the symphony of birds playing
                              to the north?

Cultivation

i.m. Eleanor Perényi, *author of* Green Thoughts

A cultivated wildness, or a wild cultivation?
Two kinds of pretence left to look natural in every garden

From next door's all the way to Sissinghurst. Would you
Adam and Eve it, the old romantic dream, or older,

To have it 'like, wild'? – but artfully done.
Horticulture, indeed – just listen to it! – for a cottage.

Here, where glorious vistas unfold the length
Of my twelve by six, I've let some branches of the rambling *Maigold*

Stay free so its waving thorns may mortify the tidy mind.
Only weeds are natural, the rest is industry.

What was the name of that American gardener years ago
who married a Hungarian baron?

She scared the shit out of the servants
By sticking her hands in it, in the flower-beds, getting right down

And dirty on her knees, unmanicuring *ante bellum*
Some lifeless park near the Carpathians.

How many levels of culture, Mr Brown, my fellow Northumbrian,
Is that? Ah yes, it was the Lady Eleanor –

When the tomato hornworms later in Connecticut
Got too gross, she scissored them in two.

It's a tough lesson in ethics, this 'not nice art' of gardening.
Is there no compromise, I'd like to know, between

The threat of Thoreau's seven miles of untended beans
And the fragrantly well-bred *Madame Pierre Oger*?

Moycullen

for Trish and Kevin Fitzpatrick

Dear friends, stay where you can see
Through, over, beyond the wires springing
By the side of the lane, beyond whatever divides.

Stay for your own sakes where you can see
Moycullen and Knockbane coming clear
Through a dubious shawl of mist,

Stay where you can see the torn white paper
Seagulls lift and totter and flit to ground
In this wind that tries to brandish all your home,

Stay where you can see the glints and sharp streaks
Of Lough Corrib as the light lifts and for a second
Melts, prinks the green land against the grey.

Alone in your house, I ponder on a gone decade,
Somewhere underground where our past is stored,
That now almost invisible Northumberland.

I listen to the rain pelting on glass
And the big wind again pulling at half-budded trees.
I'm wondering if it's grieving or roaring,

Coming in from the west where this strand of Galway
Has to meet head-on the main Atlantic charge.
Those years have slipped in and out

Too quietly like tides over the way to Lindisfarne,
Let smart cash put our old county under a crop of spruce
And tear the dark flesh off Ireland for good.

Dear friends, stay where you can see
Through, over, beyond these wires springing
By the side of the lane, beyond whatever divides

What was once all our common ground –
Let's try to thwart them wherever we can,
If not the years pressing in over our daily sands.

'Our Friends in the North'

for Eric & Julie Northey

They were like – (fists raised)
'Like what? Go on, then, like what?'

Like something this child could dance to
with such a rhythm,
the words don't matter yet,

                          it's the speech-flow
full-guttering from the back of the throat like

Like what?

Irish, Norse, Scots and burred
Northumbrian, stirred into a dancing reel
rising and falling and rising –

                        so harshly tender, luvver –
before the passion's flattened right out of it down south

'Howaay, man, hoy the bal ower heor!'
or *'The spuggies are fledged'*

And in the early years it was said
*'If you are going to talk like that
you can go to the school up the road'*

(A flat tone is generally best
for menace and threat, with no warm scurries
and hullabaloo of anything like feeling.)

Even then, not always
so *canny toon, Geordie*
for all the whisper-quiet yellow trolleys
addressed to Two Ball Lonnen,
and before them
the climbing trellised roses of scenty Moorside,
the Great North Road trams, rattling and roofless to sky

'Gissaride-onyer-bike-kidda?'
'Eee-lissen-him – gerr'im! Gerr'it-off-'im-Billy!'

I saw a window with a hole
splattered like black mud –

'Ah-seen'im-hoy-it-Mam!'

and my stomach melting
down my strengthless tiny legs

'Eee-ya-dortypig-smash'is-fyess!'
'Howaay-let's-do'im!'

What tales can you tell, canny bairn?
                              The first ones, always
in the right language.

And more than a thousand books later I was watching
moving pictures of a grey river still holy to me,
and those lovely garths and wynds climbing ancient from the Side of the
                                                                        town
with, above, the Tyne Bridge's sea-green coathanger
and my grandfather's stone towers bulking at each end

That's two per County, like

and the screen's arguing families fell out of focus –
all I could hear through the broken black hole was

Like what? Go on, then, like what?

Like words do when they dance,
like the rhythms that undo
the bindings of the heart,
                              so close to the border
it's easy to forget they were once my own.

That Other Martinet

i.m. R.G.P.
artist, architect, lexicographer (1928–2000)
and for Jennie P.

I find the Imperfect is the great tense of my life – quite an intense tense –
but it shall not at least be aoristic any longer.

John Ruskin

Ars longa, vita brevis
Seneca, after Hippocrates; typed across a postcard of
Salvador Dali's *The Enigma of William Tell* by R.G.P. in 1977

All my sentences would begin *'Richard, do you remember when…?'*
So much you taught me about art and creatures with wings
I can say now 'For all the silences between us, you enlarged my light.'
The black out there's like the imperfect black inside where
I'm staring through the window, through reflections, at the darkness
over the North Sea, rushing westwards, Sweden behind me, and memory
comes unspooling into a mess of so many frames per second:
I'm sitting still at hundreds of miles an hour in the unfinished night –
it feels like I'm rushing backwards through a relapse of fifty years
into a weird heyday of short trousers and ration-books…
Behind me, I know, you're fighting off the wheedling voices that tell you,
in the night's wee haggard hours, it's time to call it a day.

I know as well as you now this is one spring when you'll not come out
from behind your books and screens, your great tome, your monument
of a dictionary still not finished, you'll not swing (like Dr Johnson on crutches)
over the cobbled streets of Lund in search of a perfect dhal for the Bhuna
Gosht…
After years of silence when parents kept you *persona non grata*,
our letters flew back and forth – across half a life I can still recall your pages
full of Mondrian, The Soft Machine, *On the Road* and Dollar Brand…
it's non-stop, the flickering images – I'm seeing again a comma butterfly
spotted one spring in a bluebell wood, those precisely ragged wings,
the white marks underneath that say 'Pause – draw breath!' before
it heads for the shade, as all our seasons do, faster and faster,
and our hands grow dry, beating at the airy days, fluttering, failing.

Now, as my beard grows whiter and young women's voices grow fainter
from the back of the room, your older-brother's tricks
of holding me over a stairwell till I yelled for a parachute,
or guiding my hand to draw the primaries of an owl in flight
(though whether Barn or Tawny's well out of range),
come through the decades into focus in this tiny craft
of two wings and a prayer above the sea – sharp as the blue,
black and yellow stripes of your blazer I craved for years,
and more crisply than our phone chats of the 1990s.
Ten years older, you dared to tease that gruffly tender martinet of ours
for sharing Hitler's birthday – each April 20th I'd run for cover!
I forgot to say I've found that *martinet*'s the French for a swift,

apt enough for one who came back from the trenches and the fly-blown
dead...
I like this confluence of our colonel father and a bird that dozes
on its sickle wings – they seem to hold time at bay, that other martinet.
How much it cost to give your studied wave from the pillow,
I can nearly guess: we held each other's gaze a moment longer than
when you're sure tomorrows will follow on the usual midnights.
Outside, the city daffodils burned my eyes, the sky was louring.
The future perfect, Richard, 's not a tense that brings much pleasure
from anticipation, and we couldn't rewind these three days of ours
any more than one could stay Bede's sparrow from its hurry to the dark.
Time doesn't come round again like baggage on the Stansted carousel,
so I'd hate to think Seneca's *bon mot* means little more than *Buzz* and *Go*!

Settle Down

Settle down, settle down! Is this a nursery or
a garden? There's a war on, and a little one left
at play in the greenery. Even this far north

motes dance in June. The others have gone
sailing, shooting, studying, half-brothers all.
Just one left, on his knees in the weeds.

What war nature is – spikes on the fruit bushes
that mingle blood with berry-juice. Tiny rituals
behind the trellis, behind the rose bushes.

(Not yet time for the heavy petals of *Peace*
to please the colonel and his lady.)
He settles to inspection: a fresh splash of white

from a thrush, like a worm of paint from a tube,
parasols of rhubarb almost high enough
to crawl under, stalks like legs, legs like stalks,

and on the path the twisted dry knot
of a dead worm. Was it from fire? Was it
from *his* fire? What fun! The guilty sizzle

on the end of a stick? What nature war is.
He comes running from the garden, screaming,
fruit-blood gargling from his mouth all madder lake,

the tanks roaring and lifting, their tracks
screaming at air, as they circle and wheel beyond the trellis
and the trees, green skin stripped from meadow-flesh,

metal shrieking at him shrieking…
He is four, and he is practising with all his wee bravado
to leave the place he can – the place we can –

never leave, where he has learned some things
among the weeds, and fruit-seeds catch
in his teeth like stones.

Urnings

Somewhere about the time when I was
old enough to know the meaning of 'earn' –
as in 'Go to the shops for some bread and earn

your keep' – but not anywhere near sage
or old enough to understand 'urn'
as in 'burial' and the *Hydriotaphia*

of Thomas Browne, or know what poor Keats
was on about who was already dead at the age
my father went off in 1914 khaki to Flanders

(*Flanders* – what on earth were *they*?),
I heard a friend of my mother's
use, wistfully, Scotchfully, the word 'dis-

earning' about him, called up and away from home
again, trammelled this time by the disposition
of coastal ack-ack and twenty years or more

of nightmares where bits of horses, hanging,
bled for a while from trees,
and smithereens of 'Wipers' lay, crunching,

under his feet, and I just knew
'We'll have no money left now, nothing to eat
or buy me new soldiers with!'

Much later, after he was home and I was old
enough to get to know him a little, I realised
he was 'discerning' – but not much, I suppose,

before I was capable of thinking
of the meaning of meanings, and the meanings
of sounds and how they lodge

in the hedgerows and fields and paths
of memory. And why now, suddenly, do
I remember 'dis-earning' after all these years?

It's a favourite word of the curiously egregious
Thomas Browne – look at *The Garden of Cyrus* – and
I was reading his account of sperm-whales

cast up on the Norfolk coast near Wells,
and what the locals made of spermaceti:
their waxy oils, their 'questuary', he says,

(like 'getting and spending') hindered knowledge (and,
I dare say, discernment), among the soap-boilers...
and it came to me that in French a sperm-whale,

itself a misconception
and misnomer, is a *cachalot*,
or as we might say a 'cash-a-lot'...

and there it was: in a brilliant micro-second
quite the opposite of Browne's 'slow Latinity'
there coincided, collided, fused,

that pawky Scots drawl of 'dis-
cerning', a fear of empty plates and red reminders,
and my poor poor father.

Flesh Markets

We are traders too of a sort, from a safe distance.
We watch the pictures, we pay a little gelt
for our sensations and our feasting: these folks give themselves
without knowing, to those they cannot see.

(No, it is not a consolation, knowing
that if this is to be any kind of elegy, it is bound
to be forged from strangers' pain.)

Their streets are the broken trestles
where they display their wares:
it hurts them but they cannot stop,
they barter flesh for bullets,
they exchange their own meat for fire,
hoping for more land, or restored land. This is not
what we usually mean by a market.
It is not difficult to imagine the smell
that rises among the fumes of desolation.
Those with longish memories will talk of
the knacker's yard, the reek of the glue factory.

What is it about this feud that sucks back
the old words out of the mists –
massacre, carnage, slaying and slaughter,
battue, pogrom, a *noyade* in their own juices?
(There is a fearful relish in their taste on the tongue.)

Over there the butchers
cannot shut up shop now they've started,
there in the smoke-filled villages and towns
of a green and reeking land; we here cannot take
our eyes off what lies through the seemingly
unclosable doors of the shambles
that happens to be there, not here,
not on this particular pavement.

October Flowers in Prague

i.m. Doris Weisserova 17 May 1932–4 October 1944
Margit Koretzova 8 April 1935–4 October 1944

Here, in the heartland of Europe, I have seen pictures
      That come right at you like kids
Out on a free afternoon: whiter than any old paper,
      Clouds hanging in a sky of young cobalt,
A few wild spring flowers standing with imaginary
      Leaves for all the things that wild
Spring flowers stand for – these awkward pretty
      Marks of pink and yellow, and one red
Bright rose. I want to steal them all, God knows,
      Holding my breath at the butterflies above
Not so much caught in flight as always flying still
      On patchy wings as delicate as what
A child might think a soul to be, above tenderly right
      And unhurt grass. Not by years only do they transform
Continuously the nature of design, these flowers,
      The undecaying art of wings, here under glass
In the old Jewish quarter. Fifty years have passed
      Since these two girls watered their colours
In wooden dormitories. I was a child then, too,
      Chasing peacocks with a jar in a long garden.
Night was a heavy dark that pressed my open eyes
      Till they hurt. But that was all.

I have come to this now by the scenic route,
      Down the mountain road from Dresden and Teplice
Through the quick scent of pines after rain;
      I have driven myself through the streets they knew,
The leafy avenues of Terezin where heavy
      Garrison walls of golden stucco
Are showing their age in the falling baroque
      Of an August evening. But on the banks and slopes
That were platforms at the terminus I see it is only their
      Art that can tell the brightness in the grass.

Like Voluptuous Birds

i.m. Jacques Michon

What can one voice in a million do when the world
seen from this sad October island is full of the usual bloody rackets –
the blistered shrieking from unhappy rooms,

each repeated *Yes* of accommodation drowning
in the bawl of grim lives in spate? It's a rare songbird
can make your heart miss a beat and then another

and send it soaring, but you can forget about nightingales
and those skylarks we've press-ganged to stand in
for human song and a few mucky scraps we've left of beauty –

catch, if you can, this young voice when tall winds
are picking at the wooden pleats of the ceiling
or giving a rough elbow to the old hall by the Suffolk shingle,

and you'll know that this is not a voice, like some women's,
of glassy sounds unravelling under pressure:
this sound is rich and abdominal, tuned for our times

with almost-concealed art, not playing to lyric horrors,
not teasing our desperate stretching for big dreams.
This is a voice that's both velvet and poignant

like an eerie chocolate song, a voice that slides
through lunchtime and moonlight. I have been lucky
and caught this voice making magic out of French, German,

English verses, the notes rising like voluptuous birds
with that sense in the sound that shakes your temple bones,
like that soprano we heard once, years ago as if last night,

at the top of a stone tower in Prague, singing the city,
the whole nation wonderfully, into freedom.
And now this darkish, this shining voice, that comes to us

like a sheaf of water, washes us and the air clean,
and we find that, as so often when some truth is made,
quite ordinary signs have shed their shitty wrinkled skins,

words like 'wonder' and 'love' and suddenly
even 'truth' itself have dared to come back out again,
blinking, into the gingerly daylight.

(Aldeburgh, Suffolk)

Reading the Air at Southwold

i.m. W.G. Sebald 1944–2001

As I sat there that evening in Southwold overlooking the German ocean,
I sensed quite clearly the earth's slow turning into the dark.

W.G. Sebald, *The Rings of Saturn*

That was the afternoon I thought I saw him,
just a glimpse, scarfed and flitting in a dark overcoat,
glasses, bare head, hastening north along
the promenade in front of me, making for the pier
and passing on our left the strange white significance
of Southwold's inland lighthouse.

In life I'd never met him, never even seen him,
so it must have been the *Sailors' Reading Room*
and the peculiar air that moves round it
that brought him, not back but into a dimension where
I found myself believing that he had just passed
the *Lord Nelson* ahead of me, and rounded the corner

by the great black anchor. Returning, I paused,
nonplussed once more by the feature whose absence
from *The Rings of Saturn* has always puzzled me,
the tall thin signpost, whose complicated
hand-painted fingers point out the nautical miles
across the German Ocean towards The Netherlands' ports –

Zeebrugge, The Hook, and so forth. It's an unlikely omission,
a kind of untidy absence, for one who describes,
as if he had observed it himself from Gun Hill green,
the Dutch Fleet materialising out of the morning mist
for the battle of Sole Bay on May 28th, 1672.
Corpses were washed up for weeks. And one who says

he himself once fell asleep on the beach at Scheveningen,
right across the waves from Suffolk. Here on Southwold prom
he must have seen, I told myself, leaning against
the shove and blatter of the gale, that the Dutch coast
wasn't much further away than Ramsgate to the south.
If this were just a wee mite of a story, I would continue:

'It was in Ramsgate that I had first acquired
a copy of *The Rings of Saturn*...' There would be inserted
into the text a black and white image of the receipt –
an already weakening piece of evidence, certainly
not memorabilia – like the Verona pizza bill
in *Vertigo*, or the one I have for *Campo Santo*,

that reads 'Borders, Books Music and Cafe,
12–13 Market Street, Cambridge, England,
29/07/05 04.05 pm'. How defenceless
they look, these vestiges, whose blackest inks will fade
like us to nothingness. It wasn't, of course, WGS,
the 'Max' of my imagination, though I have felt

his presence more than once these past years
since I found his books – even in the four years
since his death: here in Southwold, by this modest
little brick museum, sometimes in Norfolk,
or along the Europe-facing Anglian coast
with its quirks and crumblings and isolations, places

like Shingle Street and Dunwich. And even
in Vienna, familiar to us both, where he once
hauled his depression round the streets for days till
his shoes fell apart, and he himself had a vision –
the cowled figure of Dante ahead of him in Gonzagagasse.
It was there, in the meticulous gardens at Schönbrunn Palace,

only this year, in burning September sunshine
the day after I read of this, that my companion
and I came across on a path a damaged black beetle,
its blue metallic wings so astonishing they seemed
to belong to a Queensland butterfly. And I wish I could
have told him how, one day in August, 1959,

I sat in the garden of a grand villa in Gloriettegasse,
listening to a distinguished doctor, the father of a girl
I had come to visit, recount how in his father's time
the Emperor's monkeys at Schönbrunn used to throw
their shit-balls over the wall, just where her sister and I
were sitting in deck-chairs... I stood for a while,

leaning on the rail, looking out across dirty
autumn waves seething in towards me, swirling
and spuming between the groynes, pondering on
the violence of the tide that made the sea look like
the foaming white coffee served in exhausted
waiting rooms, spewed out across the shore and

then sucked back again, like backwards-running film.
Later that afternoon I sat alone till tea time
in the bar restaurant of the Crown Hotel. The rattle
of crockery in the kitchen had long since subsided…
I was re-reading parts of section IV
of *The Rings of Saturn* in which the narrative moves

so fast you lurch and sicken, as if you're reading
too long in the backseat of the 20th century while it swerves
through its grim chicanes, here swivelling
from East Anglia's calm to Yugoslavia
in the 1940s, and the not unsayable
butchery of Serbs, Jews, Bosnians by Croatians,

with their German and Austrian confederates.
One photograph, so blurred it might be a photocopy
of old newsprint, shows a line of Monday washing
strung up with bodies inside, like those 'strange fruit'
pictures from the Deep South. In his characteristic photos,
that surprise by suddenly appearing on a page in black

and white dress instead of text, carefully made
to look a hundred years old, I am never quite
convinced that the most recent are really his: the straightforward
shot of a tombstone, say, or a view of a distant river,
always makes me believe that he was standing just
out of frame, staring back at us – a position

from which his sharpest insights, rising from grief
and memory, were perhaps so often obtained.
(So shocking is it to find on page 263
a younger picture of the author himself, leaning
against a Lebanese cedar, that it is
for some moments impossible to trust it.)

Some of them, of course, *are* almost a hundred
years old – we should not now be
so surprised by seeing the tunic jacket
of Franz Ferdinand full of blood and holes.
From those wars through which my own father
fought and somehow zigzagged safely

I turned back a page or two to get
my bearings again, in Southwold with its shrinking shore,
on a Sunday afternoon in a wintry autumn,
and found myself reading on page 96:
'That afternoon I sat alone till tea time
in the bar restaurant of the Crown Hotel.

The rattle of crockery in the kitchen
had long since subsided…' We think we know
all about the fuse lit by the son
of farmer Princip, but we go on reading the ashes
in the air, in the here and now, wherever,
as clearly as words on a page from *Vertigo*.

Down on the Cape

for Ella

View from the Table Top

for Jessica P.

It takes so little time – the surprise is not in already
nearing the top, about to step out onto that headless plateau,

but in the speed of soaring: Saturday morning's ascension
into a gaudy midwinter, the shore falling away into

patterns of city and dockyards, the Lion's Head and Signal Hill
wilting into green bumps as if, south of the tropics, I were somehow

falling in reverse, and every tone of blue from sky to sea,
some bleached to exquisitely painful white,

makes me think I'd like to be flying, out over the waves
like a plunge diver chasing after a shoal of pilchard

if only I had a gannet's eye for it, and if I weren't listening hard
to the motor heart thudding comfortably

as the little blue and white Rotair cabin like a glazed pastille
that I was ten minutes ago watching from down there

transports dozens of us to this predestination, a brief conspiracy
that everyone's in this together, swearing it's not a dream,

spirited and perspiring, and indeed inspiring each other
to soak the sweetness of every second up –

I've been thinking about this trip for fifty years, ever since
I saw the photo, brown as boot polish, in a pre-war annual

and pored over the image till it stuck like something
caught in the gaze of history, not quite irrecoverable but buried

almost as deep as speech: now it takes so little time, after all, and
there's so little time to take, the car rotating democratically –

all shall have their high-flown glimpses of Good Hope
where vision, dreams, memory are suddenly colliding on land,

tumbling over tourists and granite boulders
and dassies on tea-room tables... Free of summer's 'table cloth'

the view shows you not just where you've come up from
but where and how far you might still have to go,

in those uninsured distances of light – be careful, little girl,
as you look down from the edge of your seven years...

better to stay for a moment, as you are now,
on the boulder, arms up, chuckling, all dark for once

posing against the sun, because there's time enough
to hold my hand and look out from this very flat top of Table Mountain,

your country, not mine, across to the left, to the south east,
round the cape, the finishing point, wherever it is

that two oceans collude, east and west, settling their differences
of heat and cold, and time to wonder where they've been hiding

the mysteries of the coelacanth... And straight in front,
down there, my dear, in all that charming waste of offshore blue lies

the dark pebble of the not wholly invincible Robben Island
we might take a closer look at some other fine midwinter day.

Communication Studies

At home spotted birds like starlings and thrushes,
the crafty mimics, can get you racing into the house
to answer calls from that mobile phone
they're using to ring each other over the roof-tops.

Here at the other end of the world such larky
sophistication comes a little slower, but it comes…
or is it a different flattery that I'm reading in
meanings from my own repertoire? Impossible, even here
among the flower-farms and the vineyards,
to switch off the semiotic bells and whistles –

malachite sunbirds, whose shiny-metal feathers
switch from golden amber to *Go* in the sun
as they dance for a moment in mid-air,
start to call some very long numbers:
Hello, darling, they'll be saying,
just landing on the almond tree – anything you want?

Little black and white shrikes dive on and off
the power lines like kids in Canny Toon strip,
their guttural chirring rising like old Saturday rattles.
A jackal-buzzard, cruising the thermals
over Moores End and Mountainwood,
mewls like a hungry kitten watching us finish up
the cold beef on the terrace below,
and the pinotage sloshes out of the bottle
like a gush of warm blood.
Beyond the tennis court the rainbow hose-birds
hiss and spray, hiss and spray.

The quietest call is the measured thump of the tympanum
I can hear from deep inside the bird of paradise flower
on your black T-shirt from Kirstenbosch Gardens,
my head perched on your left breast (*O Strelitzia mia!*).
And yet. And yet. None of these is a proper songbird…
and the Cape canaries with their seemingly endless

untarnished piping from midwinter lavender will keep on
suddenly, all together, stopping —

as if they sense something rushing towards us
along the rocky tunnels of the Banhoek Valley
and the Hellshoogte Pass — as it is, this afternoon or
the unconditional silence.

Economics at 100 Tennyson Street

One of my sons has bought a house in that other East London,
down on the Cape. In such a broad thoroughfare from the heart
of the old city down to the unrepeating fretwork of surf on sky
you could once have turned round in one manoeuvre
a wagon drawn by oxen, or a regiment of redcoats.

It's DIY that makes dreams really work – cutting out the rot,
scraping, stripping, sanding, making it new – he's busy
on the tin roof slapping on coat after coat of black paint
to keep out the worst of the salt-spray from the Indian Ocean.
Now his walls are white, pristine, perhaps, so when new neighbours
pause, some black, some white, to say it's looking good,
does it make a blind bit of difference to know he's not rich
and that in this rainbow city black paint and white are half the cost
of brighter colours in Tennyson, Caxton, Longfellow Streets?

Outside the Café Mozart

Under the umbrella of a day-dream in blue-and-white stripes
it's meltingly hot for Easter and I'm pouring down
a pint of cold passion-fruit and realising that this is March 31st
(which was once my mother's birthday), and wondering if
a Viennese fiddler is about to come outside or a waitress
to launch into a little something from *The Magic Flute*, and I'm half listening
to the patterns, somehow both nasal and guttural, of Afrikaans gossip at
                                                            the next table.

I try to work out if they're talking about the election,
but the late summer sun's a killer and a fortnight's an age in anyone's politics.
A city suit a couple of tables away plumps up the ruffles
of his black, green and gold ANC rosette,
and tries to check the effect in a shop-window and whether
we're all watching him, when

slicing through the chatter come guitar chords from behind us and a voice
that's high and old, and full of pain and gravel:
it's a good shouting blues except the words are Xhosa for a verse or two
before they switch without seam or effort into
'*Baby, Don't You Do Me Wrong*' and he runs through
snatches of musicals, old pop songs, more blues quotations and finally
skips back into his own tongue… He never pauses, this old man
in a flat cap and blue boiler suit, just changes up and down
through the gears, and I see now that when he's just playing
he pushes his lower lip right up over toothless gums and upper lip,
rolling his eyes and girning like a north-country comic.

But his guitar's talking tunes from another delta –
four crashing steel-string chords and
he bows mockingly, self-mockingly, 'Yeah, *yeah*…'
He nips swiftly through the tables,
coins rattle into his cap and he's away.

Classic and simple – *get in before they notice, knock 'em flat,*
take the money, get out fast.
You could have put the whole performance on a single side
of one of those old twelve-inch shellac 78s whose whizzing surfaces
could seem to make the air wobble:
I remember from childhood a shimmer
in their blackness, as if something in a song were beginning to glow.

(Cape Town, April, 1994)

Just So Long (As)

for Barbara Segall

Ahae! *My heart is heavy with the things I do not understand.*
'Mowgli's Song' in Rudyard Kipling, *The Jungle Book*

How do you know what it is you're looking for
until you've found it? I turned sixty-eight yesterday
so I was thinking about this, as you do (though
I must say wolves had never entered my head).
Those prawns last night at *Chez Maurice* were bigger
than my fingers, still stained today with garlic and butter.

Just so. Memory, scent. No, not *that* 'this',
but *this* 'this': here come extravagant breakers,
the kind of blue that might have been rolling itself up
all the way across from Perth, the waves uncoiling
on arrival like tubular creatures turning over sideways over
and over in midwinter June, as if to unwrap themselves
from water, and then dying in the pools
with nowt to show but spots of spray, just below me here,
sipping my mid-morning *latte* on the sun terrace
of the Oyster Box Hotel, next to its own lighthouse
in red and white: this is someone else's *Pays Natal*,
though it would look just right at Whitley Bay.

(I'm writing to you from Umhlanga Rocks –
context is all!) Remembering things you didn't know
you knew is a kind of invention: coming upon something
out of a different blue, like this – reading that it was 'wolves'
leaping up at the feet of a dead man seated on a rock
on Ghost Mountain, (see *Nada the Lily*, 1892,
by Rider Haggard), that set Rudyard Kipling off down
the two-year track to Mowgli's brothers, the Council Rock
and *The Jungle Book* twice over...

                              And this is all it needed –
from Zululand to the Indian Raj in a sentence that flashed me
back to 154 Moorside North – at once the pages are riffling
like sunlight on startled pilchard or the swinging blade

of Umslopogaas, and the Forties are rushing in again,
flooding along my shoreline – *(Why does Rikki-Tikki-Tavi
never come to my pillow? What would it be like, kneading
the breasts of Ayesha?* et cetera, et cetera*)* – and just as surely,
just as beautifully, ebbing away just so sadly,
the decades bubbling and expiring… That's fine.
Just so long as you know what all this *thisness* is
when you see it coming right at you, out of the blue.

Gnomic Aorist

Gold never could keep a secret.
People love wearing sunlight
laced about their necks, circling their fingers.
You can see spoil
heaps from the plane.

Previously, there was nothing I could have compared
it with, the 'uncertain gold'
of the light on the highveld this afternoon,
round about the time of day the ladies
would have been sipping ceylon
from bone china cups
blowsy with chintz.

The shiny pallor of dead grasses,
more affluent in their tones than old gold
or white gold,
away to the limits of what you can see
has a kind of splendour that's said
to make the hearts of dutchmen melt.
I can see it now that I've had some help.

The city began with the usual lust
for bright metals and rocks, so
a few shacks, ever-deepening holes in the ground
and cheap coffins, or none,
were what came next.

My mother said she preferred the superiority
of silver, like her discreet wedding ring –
'I always thought gold looked a bit vulgar'
(though not to my father).
                              Oh, those Scots,
you'd think they never knew where
their precious metals came from.

(Johannesburg/Stellenbosch, March, 2007)

No End of a Lesson

We have had no end of a lesson: it will do us no end of good.
Rudyard Kipling, 'The Lesson'

I

The cattle, horses, goats have all been butchered
Before their eyes, the flocks of sheep are bayoneted

And left to rot across the pastures. Like late summer
Thunder-clouds, smoke palls drift overhead

From smouldering farms. The soldiers have prodded and
Herded them into cattle-wagons, the women

And children, a thousand or two eventually, and taken them
To the special camp to keep them safe

Behind barbed wire that's twice their height.
They have been carefully housed under thin canvas

On the bitter-coldest slope of the hill,
These families without men, who will not give in or give up,

Sometimes a dozen or more to a tent: despite
The warmth of numbers, they are freezing together

On the damp ground; they grow hot again, with measles
Or typhoid, and shiver even more. For the babies they get water

And degraded coffee. Every war's the same for civilians –
The usual words with their dreadful rhymes:

Mothers without brothers, daughter and
Slaughter, and, after, the screaming silence where

Once there was laughter. 'The man whose livelihood
Has been destroyed, whose wife and children

63

Have been taken from him, will lose the will to fight,'
Says General K, trusting the thickness of his presumption.

After months in this place of concentration they grow thin
As wishbones. One in five children is fading quite away.

Sometimes, they say, they come upon surprises in their rations:
Ground glass, fish-hooks, razor-blades.

II

You have seen the photographs, of course –
All skulls and eyeballs, bodies like bundles of bones
Cackhandedly wrapped in skin?

No, you have not seen them.
You have seen pictures *like* them.
The Boers of the Transvaal and the Orange Free State

Could know nothing of Belsen or Ravensbrück
Still to come, forty years down the road:
Only the designs of early British camps

Where mothers, wives, young children
In this and thirty others
Died off quickly in the heat at Christmas,

Or the freezing rains of the high veld in July –
Not forgetting, as we usually do, all the other camps
For the servants and labourers

Who were not white. They were dying too –
The invisibles in their thousands.
And what was it all for, this 'regular sort of picnic',

This final 'gentleman's war', this 'tea-time' squabble
That became a bath of blood for the new century
To learn how to swim?

Gold, of course. Isn't it always gold or
Diamonds or reserves of oil – whatever it takes
To bankroll a ravenous empire with the muzzles off?

Unless you want to say it's competing gods,
Making us mad again and again,
In the same and different ways.

III

I was thinking about all this,
Taking a breather at the entrance to the cemetery in Irene,

Peering through the bars of the locked gates,
Reading the notice of commemoration

About all the families the British buried here.
The village is just a mile or two

From Jan Smuts' farmhouse, the great old Afrikaner
The Boers didn't trust for getting too cosy with the enemy

After the war was over. Trees from far-off countries
Reach out overhead, mixing with the natives,

Dark hadedas chuck their mocking cries around,
Hoopoes are playing on the lawns of ample bungalows,

And I see in one garden a couple of midwinter sunbirds
Interrogating a honeysuckle still in flower.

The streets are wide and quiet. I turn into
Pioneer Road to visit my new grandson,

Little Alexander, already great at not-yet-two,
Dribbling a football round the pool or just smiling

With the sagacity of the very young. The properties here
Are protected by walls of local stone the colour

Of gingerbread and biscuit – along their tops run
Electric fences or razor spikes. The windows are barred.

★

Later, security guards will smile and wave me
Straight through the high steel exit gates,

Each looking in his spruce uniform like a paratrooper
From the Democratic Republic of Azania.

'No end of a lesson,' he said of that war nobody won
a hundred years ago, that no one's quite forgotten here.

True enough, but not in the sense Kipling meant, I guess.
Irene, you may remember, is the old Greek word for *peace*.

Back to the Future

'Anything Is Beautiful If You Say It Is'

Here am I in Suffolk, UK, ripping open the envelope
From Langhorne, USA, enjoying the confluence of chances that
Booksellers Tom & Rita McCauley live in Pennsylvania,
Not so far from Reading where Wallace Stevens grew up.
I have a whole row of books by him, about him, all the poetry, the letters,
Bloom and Vendler, *The Necessary Angel*, but not until today

Souvenirs and Prophecies, assembled by his daughter Holly
From the journals of his youth: some of his prolegomena,
Before he slid into his lifelong niche at the Hartford Accident &
Indemnity Co. of Hartford, Connecticut. Scraps of packing paper
Fall from the cardboard case, each listing details of
The Hartford's Mutual Funds, April, 2005… What a witty touch,

What a spirit-lifting wheeze on the part of booksellers
Who have rightly guessed that he who orders Wallace Stevens
From overseas will appreciate this teasing gesture,
An *amuse-bouche*, as it were, before the feast of Stevens.
Tom McC replies to my grateful email: *'No, we had no idea*
Stevens had anything to do with the Hartford –

My wife just uses bits of junk-mail for packing.'
I try to imagine the dry oceans of paper that must float around
The State of Pennsylvania for this to be merely coincidence.
They're souvenirs of what hasn't yet happened, prophecies
From the past, beautiful in all their desperate crumpled dullness,
like his window's lemon light and the dirt along his sill.

White Grass

Passing through one of the little birthdays
In nineteen-forty-something...
The sun was hotter than he could ever remember,
And from his lookout
He could see grass below bleached
To creamy blades, like little patches
Of dried milk, and how the afternoon

Would stretch out in front of him
Along the branch he was looking
Down from, into the fly-rimmed eyes
Of the cows looking up without despair,
Their jaws rolling sideways
On and on... and he could not imagine
How he had ever got here,
Or indeed how he might
Get back down, even now.

Straight, No Chaser

I should like the Alps very much if it were not for the hills.

John Spence, 1730

Me with my scarlet runners, the know-nothing
ski-tyro with speed-lust, hits the invisible
overnight ice patch and awed bystanders watch
no ordinary sight – my aerial pirouette
like a propeller without a plane about to hit
the nursery slopes of Chesières-Villars...
Somewhere above the Dents du Midi the gods,
those misconceived tyrants of the upper air,
must have been so astonished by my lack
of serious hubris they let me off with a cracked
ankle and half a kilo of plaster that came in handy
(as it were) for my demonstration of iambics
on the way – *di-dum, di-dum* – for a few beers
down at the Cendrillon Bar.

And twenty years later those capricious clowns
quite failed to punish me on that night when
I sped down a frozen slope in Furness
under a full January moon, rocking and rolling,
flat on my back on a heavyweight plastic sack,
the glassy air and the cold beyond any sense
of whither or whence – the whizzing was one long
long vodka draught of coming down off the high
of the hill, smashing into the buffers of softer snow:
the whole gang of us, helpless and legless,
capturing moments from beyond the how or why
of somewhere to the north of now...
Dissolving at once, of course, the moments.

But let twenty more years pass and I can still reach it
at will, that half-pissed hurtle through air that nips
like an alpine *piste* – lying back again for the rush
of ice and spirit... That's the way to go, down into
the comfort and smother of the downy snow.
The teeth of the snarling cold are sharper now, though,
each time I do it, the moon's just a poignant sliver,
and I'm travelling quicker.

Jammy

Five little imitations, or wooden
Intimations of killing, much redder than raspberry jam
Or the bright arrow-marks advancing across

The map of France in my father's atlas;
Pointy-headed in their brass cylinder jackets
Squeezed into a charger clip – five of them I found

Near the base of a silver birch, I think it was, each one
Longer than my little-fingers – the colour of rich
Cochineal, but it was fresh blood I thought of then

As if they'd been used already, like arrow-tips just yanked
From warm bodies, or, worse, when I couldn't sleep,
Five little stumps brought to points with a pencil-sharpener.

('In the end you will tell us everything!')
Biggest thrill in seven years, those five little beauties,
Practice bullets for loading a Lee-Enfield .303.

My elder brother said *'Dead jammy, you finding them!'*
Better any day than some tatterdemalion bloodstained hanky
Sported like a medal ribbon for distinguished service

On the battlefields of childhood... Didn't know it was
All over by then, the war in Europe. *Vive la France!*
They stayed for decades in my bashed white Glucodin tin

With other precious martial parts – the silver Cameron Highlanders
Cap badge and the slightly rusty key to a German tank.
They leap to attention now, those little beauties, when I see

A woman open her bag and twist the shiny cylinder,
Smearing that bloody *Rouge Dior* over heavy lips, care-
Fully, massaging them together, giving a little *moue*

Into the mirror. *Vive l'enfance!* Jammy. Mortal.

Last Reel at the Essoldo

She's a terror when she threatens to leave for good and all,
that *Mnemosyne*, and take my memories with her…
Yesterday, when it was 25 in the shade, she gave me
a black umbrella, and at once I was reversing, backfiring
away into the far-off past, and then back here again:
I'm coming out of the Essoldo Cinema into Westgate Road,

Newcastle's own little Wardour Street, the rain is fair
stotting off the pavement and I'm fifteen and Gene Kelly,
humming out of tune, tripping myself up in
the gutter's overflow, arm round a lamp-post…
That brick and sandstone *Palace of Dreams* and glittering
nightmares opened, like me, in '38, but already

I've outlived by nearly twenty years its art deco mirrors
and blue enamel name with the double-S poised like
the legs of Cyd Charisse. I still carry scars from
that tremendous cavern where I see all of us
straining our pale mushroom faces towards the raging light
when the fire chases Bambi through the forest,

and I end up on the floor screaming silently,
making myself blind. We could work out how other cinemas
got their names – all the classic flavours, Olympia, Regal, Apollo…
even Odeon. But *Essoldo*? Before he could be reduced
to a number, Solly Sheckman (b. Poland 1891) made it here
and gave his girls stellar billing in his empire of lights –

Esther, **Sol**ly and daughter **Do**rothy. From such trivia come
the time-travelling tricks, the teasing affluence of memories,
these unreliable movies telling us we have lived our lives
somehow. That last week, before *THE END* came up
for real, they showed, as if it were the be-all and
end-all for everyone, a re-run of *Back to the Future*.

New Designs from the Autumn Catalogue

Greetings, dear *lecteurs* of the green and discomposing world
on this, the last day of September! Profits are tumbling like seeds from my
black hollyhocks, the same ones Jefferson grew at Monticello –
'of a darke red like black blood,' as John Parkinson said in 1629.
The rain has fallen down, and stopped. The watering-can is avid
and scarlet: you hold its tail and pour from the beak.
The garden is full of noises. From the lime-tree, haunt of finch and spuggy,
the jackdaw *kraaarks* twice, and Poppy the bull terrier
and Maudie the black pug are barking madly, perhaps because
the doorbell and the telephone are, nevertheless, as silent as
my late mother. The low-down sun is tired now but still warm-hearted,
and there's a yellow leaf suspended like my disbelief
from a single spun thread, turning, turning in the clockwise
anticlockwise air… choosing… refusing… This is a temporary arrangement,
unlike my mother: the ruddy corvid comes from Ikea – is it
half empty or half full? My mother, who is late, who was not from Ikea,
who has no options, was barking much of the time, I used to think.
The huge tree is merely droning, like the line to Customer Relations
until it says suddenly 'Buy Buy!' These words are twirling
on threads in my brain. William Blake calls from my china mug
'Help! Help!' and a terrific arm is stretching up – all you can see –
all you can hear now – from the turbulent waves, on the table
in the green metal garden. *'Ahae! My heart is heavy*
with the things I do not understand,' said Mowgli to me yesterday.

There may be too many pages here, glittering with transferred epithets.
Is that the polliss I hear, come to get me for exceeding the ration
of pathetic fallacies? *'Ah'm sayin' nay more ter ye till*
Ah've spoeken ter me execkitive,' said Adam once upon a time
in his Byker allotment. I repeat them, confident that with these words
the cherry and plum flowers of the fuchsia will cry and cry enormously,
with a loud pleasure, at least till October has changed its tune. I mean,
there must be something fresh, instead of just *'The price of admission*
is eternal acquisition.' Retail it to me, please, Maudie,
from the garden, you lovely black pudden with googly eyes.

You want more variety? You want something more than common or
garden?
Check out that sumptuous bouquet at a German supermarket
near you… 'BOGOF! BOGOF!' they cry as they twist our arms.
We see yet again how the catalogue offers sumptuous rhetorical questions:
are we to resist, and refresh the lifetime shopper's almanac
with the credences and sensible ecstasies of the imagination?
Trust this above all, or else the daw, black or scarlet,
and the cushat without his collar may never again come calling,
with their sad and bonny cries, on the falling gardens of our selves.

All she wanted, Phyllis, was to make things, to make things grow.
I see this now that I have, once again, hastened too slowly.

The Peppered Moth, Among Other Things

for Eric & Julie Northey

(i)

I have not forgotten that day when we walked
the Freemen's Meadow with Bessie chasing
the long wooden stick-bone as we went through our old paces,
out on the Sudbury water meadows –
and over us the heavens were slow-raining ash and
smouldering smudges of charcoal, while the breeze
pushed at accumulations of dirty-silver cloud over the town,
not unlike the aftermath clouds of devastation
you'd think might blow over
when a war has passed already across a landscape.
Here and there on rising ground the fields flared up, as bright as
patches of rape flowering through smoke.

Practical men, farmers. They could spend a day or two in those times
burning off the stubble, and they'd have no reason to imagine
what all that drifting ash might make others think of, what kind
of 'second mowing' might come with the territory of *aftermath*.
New to these parts then, I wrote afterwards that these bodiless shards
of August were like 'those flakes memory planes free from shadow,
things I've read of further back than '76, ash-down risen from
distant chimneys where the fires did not smell of eucalypt or wheat'.

(ii)

Imagine, if you will, a white
moth, four little flakes of wing
so milky that you could conjure them to
a vanishing point on a porcelain plate, almost.

Now, taking the grinder with black pepper –
I won't, for obvious reasons, say 'black pepper pot'
because this one is a pretty phallic *Silverado Special* –
turn it upside down and let gravity and the battery-powered ceramic grinders

deliver a smattering of spicy grit over
the milky wings… and some more…

Et voilà! The Peppered Moth. *Biston betularia,*
that is to say, if we are dining with entomologists.
Now imagine that you keep swivelling your wrist
as if trying again, without demanding exertion,
the handle of a locked door (perhaps into
a room where dreams are incarcerated
without your being sure of bliss or nightmare).
Before long the falling pepper will have obscured
all that was white on the wings.

And now imagine that the pepper pot is not
for pepper, forget the silver – it's really a model chimney,
the industrial kind you could have seen in Manchester about 1850
when Manchester was called 'the chimney of the world',
and what you are depositing on the moth is not pepper
but soot, making, as it were, a carbon copy.
This is still a Peppered Moth, but now it's *Biston carbonaria,*
the melanic version, dark as the underside of a peacock butterfly.

You were just imagining the pepper pot, after all: what created
the black Peppered Moth is called 'evolution' by everyone
except those who were born yesterday,
and believe the earth was born two or three days before yesterday.
(They belong to a group called the *Clouded Vapourers*
who fly straight from the dark into
the glare of misunderstanding, without passing through
an intervening stage of enlightenment.)

One last time: imagine the trees of Manchester
a hundred and more years ago,
dyed black as the sooty buildings –
no pale peppery-looking lichen
clings, unpoisoned there, to oak or beech.

And imagine the pale version of our moth
alighting on a grim crust of bark –
it might as well let its dotty wings go all fluttery
and call *Come and get me!* to the ravenous birds.

Generation after generation in the Black Countries
of Victorian England, this moth turned from speckled white to
its adaptive dark and, as if they'd learnt the concept
of belt and braces, or how to avoid the quick dash

from creation to cremation, both forms now fly
where no high chimneys obliterate the sky
for the time being.

(iii)

We, on the other hand, are much slower
to learn anything from making our skies grow
unnaturally dark over the shambles of other people's cities.
We're brilliant at inventing
lenses that switch from clear to dark in sunlight,
but we've forgotten the days when a war could last for Thirty Years.

And although it was just the day before yesterday when he made them
we have learnt nothing from Anselm Kiefer's burning books:
he wanted us to remember how easily the trees of the forest,
their branches and leaves, the beeches of Buchen, for example,
could be burnt to a cinder along with much else.
So more than forty years after the book-burning bonfires
that had once before enflamed the nightmares
of Heinrich Heine and in 1933 brought the smell
of smouldering Asch and Klee and Marx,
he made a book out of beechwood, whose pages, whose leaves,
were the leaves of beech trees,
and he burnt it till it was a cinder in the solid shape of a book.
He called it *Cauterisation of the Rural District of Buchen.*

Six in Sepia

Bright Cloud

after Samuel Palmer: 'The Valley With a Bright Cloud' 1825

There is a place where Contrarieties are equally True.
This place is called Beulah.

William Blake, *Milton*

Is it supposed to be *Good* (or *God*) *in everything*
               like silver linings,
      and all the better without any people?
I can't see it myself. *Non in Arcadia ego*, I think:
              not much in the blackened trunk
of that felled tree,
                stranded like a dead whale,

             nor in the murky stream
      winding forth and back into the distance
between trees and buildings so grim

that this might as well be a slow route to doomsday
            as the distant hill-top bastide,
and not in the maggoty silhouettes
          on the horizon (horse, waggon, cow)…

On second or third thoughts, however –
          at least that many, to give Mr Palmer
his due – perhaps, yes, in the pair of thrushes centre-stage,
          spotted with tunefulness and
              billing like doves,
                   and more likely, if at all,

in the voluminous bubbling up of
         cumulus over the valley, like extra helpings
            from some irrepressible confectioner,
to countervail a world too much cross-hatched in
          cuttlefish brown and lamp black –

a substantial exuberance, as if a spectator
of that dismal slice of Kent had said aloud
'For heaven's sake, lighten up!' or *'Mehr Licht!'* or
        'Beulah, peel me a cloud off
           that May horizon!' and
                Beulah, transcendentally, obliged
      with a great *whoosh!* of creaminess

           as if inspiration were as easy to come by as such
              cauliflowering brightness.

Early Morning

after Samuel Palmer: 'Early Morning' 1825

for Jemimah Kuhfeld

Under the oak-tree
              shaped like a field-mushroom
     which keeps off the full dazzle
of the rising sun
          the hare on the path
pauses without fear to tweak an ear to
      the distant family in the field doing
who knows what at this hour of the day
          if not saying their prayers –

they are too far off to hear
       the pair of lovebirds who one day
           held the foreground unconcerned under Palmer's
roiling cloud of cream,
             now canoodling on a twig
stuck out like a pencil
      from the hellishly black trunk of the oak-tree that's
        shaped, now that I look at it again,
more like a darning-mushroom
        over which the bright needle
      might repair the day
          from its nightly wear.

Late Twilight

after Samuel Palmer: 'Late Twilight' 1825

Hold up your right hand in front of your face
cupping it to make a backwards-facing C:
      and up against the darkening sky

         in that interlude of twice-light
            when the last of the set sun
     is going under by the minute
let it glow, into a waxing sickle moon:

               just highlights now
in the gathering-up of the day, a scatter of trees,
       a stream edged with plants and flowers,
     cottages on the skyline, his usual
fallen tree-trunk, stooks of late summer corn
     and a three-barred gate.
                What I would have liked
to ask Mr Palmer is this: 'Why have you made so exactly
        the faces of the two comfortable sheep
over whose backs
     the shepherd is stretched
       in a deep pastoral snooze

look like forbearing owls?'

O Shine That Field

after Samuel Palmer: 'A Rustic Scene' 1825

Rush of the day's first
blaze of gold –
        above the dark wood
the hill also rises
    in a balance
of night and day, and
neither, quite.

The ploughman has drawn lines
        across the acres

as Samuel Palmer is re-inventing
        with pen and brush the dream
        that will grow familiar, this amateur of Kent,
of its dimples and hollows and
                buxom little hills.

The pen, quicker than the plough, makes
its verses and reverses,
                delimiting leaves
        and twigs and seeds
of illumination
        (the mind in mid-spin); 1 – 2 – 3
apples on the branch as summer
        has begun its late turn towards sepia –
                so maybe three kinds of knowledge here
                and each one is love.

He leans forward, the ploughman, over
the faithful conjugation of the beasts, each docile ox
        under the sickle of the weakening moon
        as if he might be saying to them
'We're ready, but we'll not go yet,'
as if each day we could expect his
        sight of harvest if only
we believed more – believed enough
                in our terrain, our presence and
our maybe's perishable days.
                        Palmer knew for sure
        his God was in the cuttlefish ink, and in
the motion of the pen, and in the corn
        thick-packed under his hand.

The Valley Thick With Corn

after Samuel Palmer: 'The Valley Thick With Corn' 1825

Too bright, seemingly, for
twilight and a harvest moon,
too pale and bleached
for sunshine butters,
the light's enough for that
reclining reader
of the foreground, bedded down
in standing corn.
This particular scene doesn't
need or couldn't take the shit and
beggars of the given world –
Palmer's passionate pastoral
reveals Arcadia is also Eden is
also in his seven-by-elevens
the plump and curvy
farm-acres of Kent:
tidy stooks, chestnuts
like cauliflowers at midnight,
fences as neat as bracelets,
the herdsman's crook nothing
but a wee interrogative against
the sandy road.
Way behind them a spire
points to the pair of birds
across the stitched moon.
This could well be one of
those laughing valleys
of the psalms: the sheep
at the pool, two cows
lumbering through stubble,
the reader, there, still reading
his good book where
something must surely have been written
about clouds and their fatness,
about the counties of Albion.

When a Wood Has Skirts

after Samuel Palmer: 'The Skirts of a Wood' 1825

Below the outstretched arms of
    the crepuscular chestnut
Palmer's shepherd is piping
the passing of the day – it has to be the finale

of the pastoral, you feel, or at least this
    particular *shtick* in the classical routine,
        here in this darkness so ravenous
            it could eat your breath up.

And these are the blooming skirts
of an extravagant wood,
a jungle of a wood, branches exfoliating like mad…
And is that a *doppelgänger* sitting
just behind the piper,
            or maybe his girl?
And why are the roots twisting like pythons, why
do those leaves look like feathers?

There are shadows and silhouettes here
among the trees whose glooming shadiness
has borrowed from gothic visions
leaves and crooked arms so lurid
    they must be true –

they are precisely where the devil
    lives in his luxurious details.
So much ink to escape prettiness! So much
obscurity it's a wonder we can still make out
        the other shepherd in the distance,
leaning on his crook on the edge of – is it really a cliff?
The trees are swollen and writhing, or bizarrely
    straight and narrow poles,
the cottages threatening in their cosiness…

and suddenly you notice there are tree-shadows
and highlights all over the place,
        in the wrong place – that is to say,
too close to the source of light.

What can be more
        disconcerting, here under the skirt
                of the wood, than misplaced shadows?

So, then, how do
you read the nest
        in the crooked arm of the chestnut, above
                the piper's head?
        Is it confirmation of nightmare, or solace?

One of his favourite thrushes is watching over
        three nestlings and
                a handful of perfect eggs.

A Fig of Consequence

I feel here a most grateful relaxation and am become once more a pure quaint crinkle-crankle goth...
Samuel Palmer, at Tintern Abbey, 1835

Context is all!
            I admire him for taking
the fig here
        over the Abbey –
                    in a summer-scruffy garden
may be found as much, more, interest
        as in bare-topped ruins: so rejecting
                the easier gothic shot at the sublime
        he found it in pink hollyhocks
and a high green fig-tree,
            red tiles, grass and
                    open windows.

        This is a scrupulous little sketch
of our past, in pencil, brown ink and little
            glances of coloured water
        that dry into sensations.

And especially the foregrounded
stretch of wall:
            half a dozen lines
of free verse flattish stones
        (like wonky bricks but not at all
haywire, not artless)
            resting on bigger chunks below.

Most of it looks pretty dry, pebbles prodded into
        crumbling gaps, though some parts on the left
and near the top have had a little
            of Palmer's pale gouache
washed over them – that mortar which brings
        'a mingling together
in which the distinction
                of stones
                    were almost lost'.

86

It's the cottage face of history:
                           he shows me here
not a great arch,
                           nor ivy trellising windows
tracing a capital R for romantic,
but like Wordsworth elsewhere on the Wye
'a plot of cottage-ground'
                           'green to the very door'.

How much we want our lives on
          firm footings, and how the years
are bound together
                    with our own impassioned mortar,
and how it may crumble
                    as memory goes blundering
                              through the decades
in search of aberrations
                    that might not be.
          And he shows it
with such a delicate
                    judgement
                              of omission

that the house beyond and the intricate light and
          shadow of the leaves
                    nearly begin to look overcooked
while he turns his seeing
          into a truth
                    with little absences of the pen.

The wall's holding up
                    the edge of the garden and
          holding itself together, it's fashioned old and fine,
                    and above it on this higher ground
he leads us back through
the deliciously unmanicured bunching
          summer grass,
                    the weeds,
                              the shrubs,
          past the sapling and the hollyhocks to

the house at the back of the picture
with the green, almost roof-high fig,
a fig of consequence,

under which any of us could sit
without wanting or
waiting for any other kingdoms.

Darkness Inside Out

'Mr Blake, Mr Blake!' I shouted. 'Teach me
how to understand the peepshow of the star-pricked
heavens you write of, the patterns in the wheatfields
with their million listening ears, the sheep-faces
that will look like forbearing owls, the speech-
curve of the crescent moon and the invisible song
that gushes from the thrush's beak all spotty with tune
somewhere in the sepia skirts of the wood!'
And Mr B. fixed his grey eyes on me and
said, 'Do you work with fear and trembling?'
And when I said 'Yes,' he replied, 'You'll do!'
I said, 'Mr Blake, is it true that you played
Adam and Eve in your garden here as if Peckham
were after all radiant, reading aloud *Paradise Lost*,
the two of you, in full undress?' Laughing,
he said not – 'But you must learn to read
with fresh-open eyes if you will find your way,
to read every thing, not just books and words.
He will read for ever, and a day longer,
who wishes to see the darkness turned inside out.'
And I had this picture in my head of a valley,
fields as thick with corn as pages of words,
and a man lies reading there – one of those bosomy
valleys of Kent which I believe must be related
to the laughing valleys of the *Psalms*.
What he reads will say, 'Thy clouds drop fatness' –
all over my lovely counties that could be Albion if
only I knew better how to make the fields laugh
and sing. The stones at the bottom of the stream, even.

Pepper's Ghost

for John Pepper

I'm glad you asked me that… Some days I think I'm Jack Nicholson
squinting through the venetians in his swanky office in *Chinatown* –
that's before Polanski gets up his nose with a knife
and there's blood everywhere. What a film! – the greatest *noir*
made in colour, and the sharpest critique of capitalism the slick and
greedy lunks of Hollywood ever let slip: art concealing art,

except for the blood. I'm looking at a rose bush, green splotched with claret.
But this isn't L.A. I observe my rituals, out in the garden studio:
Richter's busy, sublimely so, with Beethoven, or Peterson with Gershwin,
I work through the South African birds on my screen-saver,
I re-read 'The Planet on the Table' and throw down my pencil again.
What are we if there's no dream-time? The cold rain shall rain.

I watch my visiting blue-tit killer-drilling at himself
in the brass door-plate: I reckon he gets around
more than I do now, arriving every 2 minutes 43 seconds during daylight.
He must hate what he sees, and his little pencil-point beak grows blunt.
Would he do this if he had imagination, if he knew who he was
and what the chances were of more fine music tomorrow?

O Tempora time – I have learnt that the president of Iran
wants Israel smashed off the map, that Tutankhamen liked a big
gutsy red, a pinotage from the pyramids (it was a good year, the 1352),
that Tony Blair's closest allies were Bush and Berlusconi the Benitophile.
Not just allies – *close friends!* Well. These bloody Bs will do for us all.
In Italy they called our prime minister *The Sultan of Bling*.

When it grows dark I'm everywhere by lamplight – in the window,
the screen: I stare at myself, reflection on reflection,
and through myself at the branches, the gestures
of the leaves not waving at me. So I *can* see through myself
while my insubstantial self, or one of my selves,
is still there, looking back, this me, or that me, and not for the first time

I wonder if there's much more to me than some Pepper's Ghost
in a Theatre Royal about 1870, all tricksy with plate glass, Hamlet's father
muttering to himself, 'Mind the gap, son' and the actor well offstage.
At the end of this narrow little street, high up where most people miss it,
there's an old name-plate, not-very-white letters on dark blue:
PLOUGH LANE, it says… followed by *a full stop!*

It's a bad sign, that, don't you think?

                                       Oh well…

never mind, here's Oscar again, and he's so good with George –
I was Doing All Right
                  They All Laughed
                              Shall We Dance?

S'quim & Stuff

For Lorna Tracy

One thing leads to another – laughter, terror – when we open our mouths,
Hustle our lips, music our tongues into shaping air, though even the
briefest word-
Journey may finish quite elsewhere, with intention left as a dodgy outpost
Of Melancholia. But the intrigues of speech – yes, irresistible as turning
a page...

Way outside my tongue's Indo-European comfort zone, there's a Bella Coola
Indian word up in British Columbia made from a squeeze-box of consonants,
Thirteen without a vowel, for when you need to say *'He used to have*
A dogwood plant'... and further south I hear that Sequim, a little town

On Washington's north coast, has an *E* so quiet you can't pick up the softest
Exhalation from it, even when the gulls have stopped their zestful massacre
Of early evening calm... The name's a corruption, of course, like so
much else
Since George Vancouver of Lynn Regis brought Cook's *Discovery*

Round these straits and creeks on a mapping cruise, looking to flag up
An island for German George III. Young Peter Puget was aboard and got
to give
His name to the nameless Sound – even so, what had been Dutch or
French was lost
Under a coat of English gloss... Languages get mucked about anyway

(*Pewjut*, not *Poojay*), but all those later decades of chicanery and bloodwork,
Importing booze and poxes and the rest of the killers, of trying to stamp out
The tongues and lore, even the spirit worlds, of people who'd treated
Their patch of earth and its creatures with decent care for thousands of
years... Well,

That's way beyond corruption, even if some of it might have been plain
Incomprehension, among all the clattering and swooping that came tumbling
As if upside down or sideways-backwards from mouths on every side –
Sounds *can* pour together into a hot confusion, as waters can, as colours can,

Even the multifarious greys and all their relatives, the tribal members
Of not-quite-greyness out across the bay of Sequim where that old Shootist
From Tinseltown used to sail his yacht, the *Wild Goose*, north-west from
                                                             Puget Sound,
Then head off along the Strait of Juan de Fuca towards the dipping sun...

What a confection, that blowsy minesweeper from World War II!
He's long gone, the big tough guy who played fighters, but felt guilty
                                                             he'd never
Fought for his country except to win the West, in battle after fake-bloody
                                                             battle
Against 'Red Indians'... now you can see the tips of masts teetering and

Fidgeting in the *John Wayne Marina*. The lawyer who later bought the *Goose*
Swore that the ghost of the Dook would prop up the bar in his cowboy hat
Or tramp the deck at night, chasing memories of *Fort Apache* past Cape
                                                             Flattery
Out into Pacific waters... On the port side he'd have passed Mount Olympus

(Home of the great god Thunderbird), and Sappho in the rain-forest, and
                                                             the mouth
Of the river Pysht – but not, I'm sorry to say, Humptulips, too far to
                                                             the south,
With all its possibilities, its ambiguities and aspirations, its plosives and
                                                             labials that
Remind us of speech itself. And of love too, since one thing leads to another.

STILL A WAY
FROM
GOOD HOPE

(Stellenbosch, RSA, 1998 – Suffolk, UK, 2005)

Snowman

It's the tiny cracked seeds of paradox
that bring savour, like cardamoms, to the *olla-podrida*
of each day, spicy, slightly gritty, among even

the most fortunate dish of onions, sweet
peppers and the dark corners of aubergine...
like the meeting, wherever, of parallel lines,

or an April that says it's autumn in a southern republic,
the poles of a continuum bending in
like a daily horseshoe of pleasure, the sun

crashing on his pale head and shoulders
this Christmas Eve. There is no end to
his distrust of the obvious,

that black might be white or vice versa,
that the light from the moon is really the benefit
of sunshine, that next month cannot

not be two-faced. And yet, the kumquat exists
and the passion-fruit, nominally blithe. He can cheat
by dreaming, he thinks, lying in the dark,

one ear humbled by the outrageously
confident snore of his companion.
Every day Christmas comes! Can you believe it?

Every day there are presents and treats
for Christmas the alsatian when she comes to the door
smiling and wagging her tail. It's quite something

to be able to smile in the dark
where no one can see the smile or the shade of skin
or the beads of sweat or the tears, and not

to fall off the planet ten times a night.
Sometimes the snowman lasts longer
than anyone expects. (Easter, 1948, anyone?)

Accept the kilter's gone. Is that best? So many stars,
so many stars everywhere,
so why the dark, ever?

Mountainwood

(on the Hellshoogte road, and the way to Languedoc)

1

The house is high up, so high
up the twisted track where the tyres
stot off ruts as hard as ironwood,
that the buzzard, quartering its patch,
rapt, hungry, single-
minded, is way below him too,

not only the unblinking over-bright
mid-morning sky.

2

No twitcher. Something of a spectator.
It was a relief not to have to
look upwards at those heavens for the time being, all that
azure, cobalt, cerulean, whatever, all that glaring
waste of time –
and those stupid puffy little clouds, for God's sake! –

but beyond them, into the mansions of milky distance
that drive star-gazers beyond themselves,
hot after pulsars and black holes… Imagine!

3

'It's not lilac, my dear,
            but jacaranda in the garden,
brought from the Americas, I believe…
            still, it is famous
for breaking hearts, in the rain
            or no, with that aching tone
absorbed into the coarse felt of
            memory in bitter weather…'

A bruising cadence, the petals falling
over the lawns of Mountainwood

4

Ingrates labour at plenitude, we anglo-saxons and celts
in a muck sweat of pleasurable guilt
when faced by the instruments of excruciating hedonism.
Can't scarper from its shiny prongs!

5

Still, it *is* a present, the day
and there's no getting away from it.
Start with the well-intended promises of breakfast –
a salad of fresh fruits on the sideboard
(papaya, nectarine, orange, passion-fruit, lychee
swim in enough sweetness to sate
any ripe Sultana's douce propensities),

still-warm breads of different shades –
fingering grain and crust, he thinks of races mixing
like flour. (Come to that, might he now be thought
to be bran, like Alison en route to Canterbury, all flour –
flower, indeed – devoured long ago? Quite preposterous.)

He could let the specially small chatter
of little girls fall past him
like crumbs to the floor.
And loaf about among
the spears of strange grass so far as
the content of his heart would let him.

> (*Regardez, M'sieur, regard ze mess
> you 'ave made!* The embarrassment
> of epicures. What will he do
> with three sets of cutlery so early in the day?
> But that was in a distant elsewhere.)

He viewed the egg-yellow muffins (so-called)
with a good imitation of 'grave suspicion': the colour
of childhood's dried egg
but the flavour, texture – unsurpassable! Compliments to... etc.
But why freckled with tiny black seeds
that fell onto his plate?

They looked like dead minutes
lying there, the past all white,
wiped clean of joy
and misdemeanour.

6

The golden sugar in the spoon mounted
above the edges – he paused and let half
tip back into the bowl.
Urge, suppression, satisfaction? No, not really.

He did not want time, this time, to move
any more quickly. Somewhere
the apportionment will be printed
like her sweet-coupons in a green ration-book.
The war's over, don't you know? Aunty's dead.
Short commons! A week's delight gone
in five minutes. (Chocolate, i.e., not the other thing.)

7

Hhmmm.
Know that Dali painting where the figure
has a backside so far behind him
it needs to be propped up on a stick
(like a brilliant future
or a six-foot prick – should that be 'with'? Tacitus says no.)?
L'Enigme de Guillaume Tell, indeed.
His brother once sent him a postcard of it, typing over
'Ars longa, vita brevis!' Ho, ho, ho.

His other message was more pertinent:
'*The lyf so short, the craft*
so long to lerne.'

Even here in plentiful Boland.
That's *Boerland* when you say it.
As in *boor*, and some dogged spadework
in the dictionary will set the cat
among the connotations.

8

The life now standing on platform…
Questions, questions: which train
was called Time, and which Life?
He could see the other one alongside clearly
(his tenth birthday just behind him),
but which one's moving? Which one
was he on? Why was there no one else
in the compartment?

The Flying Scot was flying in sepia,
building up steam, through Northumberland,
heading for the Border, tum–ti–ti–tum and 'the postal order'…
the red and black seating scratched at his
almost bare-faced cheeks

when the whistle blew
when the whistle blew

Such a waste.
Such a waste of time, like trying
to eat lettuce leaves with a spoon –

'*Use your fingers,*' she said,
'*Or your tongue… Aaah, that's better!*'
Or was it '*bitter*' she said?

9

He held the black coffee a second
or two longer than usual in his mouth
before swallowing. *Christmas
is hot this summer*. Sometimes, like now,
he put his hand to his face
and touched his cheek or lips.
They were more than warm. He really
must be present. His self, or most of it. Below the table
he wiped his finger-tips
on laundered linen.

He wished he knew more
about time and space, in Africa
or anywhere. All that stuff about 'two hours ahead'...

An hour ran past while he thought about it – he saw its tail
disappearing down a hole

10

Later, later.

He would sit on the verandah
and open himself to Mountainwood's presents
in the sun: the cupped stone hands of the valley,
grey escarpments like limestone, outcrops
of forest and woodland, periods of green delirium where
unknown cuckoos call to each other, send messages,
have conversations.

Foreground: a single gum-tree,
sage eucalypt exquisite in foliage and papery trunk.
Secretly drinking up all the water
and robbing the proteas.

'... *and their warm fields
          return no more,
              where then is paradise?*'

See, there's Farmer Vin
sharpening his axe!

Background: the stubby finger-ends
of high ground.

And the open palms of the valley-floor below
displayed fields like big allotments,
a reservoir, the intricate
straight brocade of vineyards,
terra cotta roof-tiles, and the odd
blinding flash from new gal. –

it came to him, the gal., the sudden flash
from another continent more than twenty years wide,

that mad neighbour in Sydney
who'd start about six on a Sunday morning
hammering a new roof on.
What was he called again?

> *It's twenty years*
> *but I have a long memory,*
> *Colin Coventry, you bastard!*

It was Thornleigh, the year
the bushfires came to the end of
the street in a blizzard of black flakes and
we filled the gutters with towels soaked
in cold water…
the hottest Christmas in twenty years.

And the beautiful new
> *roof shone in the sun*
> *all Sunday long*
> *all Sunday long*

> *Sing me another*
> *sweet colonial song*

11

For the moment, he thinks

if he were not essentially ephemeral, the observer, such beauty
would be appalling in its obviousness — fortunately
the eye cannot freeze-frame for ever the sun-lit rubies, the glassy
green-shine, leaping from the shrubs where the sunbirds potter.
Even that jacaranda's explosions of violet smoke
avoid banality only by the daily
as if dutiful

                petal-fall.

The greatest stories, the peaks of narrative art,
are made in melting wax
and its consequences.

I suppose that's what happens
when people rhyme banal *with* anal.

12

The tourist did nothing but fidget on a green quarter-deck.
He strolled about, lay on the grass, sat in the shade
and pestered himself. A bird laughed in the bush.
Which would come first: a glimpse
of the rusty streamers of the paradise fly-catcher
he'd waited days to see?
Or a black statistic from the *Cape Argus*
(say, one-in-four out of work and out of hope),
working its way into the foreground, niggling,
rubbing raw?

In his bedroom above the verandah
the maid on her knees would be polishing, again,
the highlights in the gleaming floor,
tidying the carelessness
of sock and shoe and grubby pants.
What might he transcribe into

the future perfect, the children
braying from the pool, the complexities
of cascading spray and sunlight,
labourers strolling through loud thickets of idiom, the smell
of bok charring on someone's *braai*?

Now there's a thought: not very far away
a small fragment of blackened bone has just
been found to have doubled
the history of *homo habilis*.

Between the holding and the letting go
he feels his days stretching into
a thinner stint, southern minutes proving in their warm
and liquid escape no different from the jerkier
movements of northern passage.

Nowhere, nowhere so many
surprises, Africa.
And Africa in all of us.

13

Still, it is definitely a present, this day,
though like all such days
it has risen into the present saturated
with ambiguous light, a daze
of this and that, the residue of all
its other days with the little curlicues of
remembered delight left attached, as well as
the black pains that rip and turn vermilion
like the whole cartilage of a life giving way.

14

Later
he promised himself

(while trying not to think that such promises,
such self-invitations, might hint at a different lingo

of aims, objectives, mission statements, about
permission, commission, submission, emission,
line management, where self-service slips out from the obfuscation
of learning outcomes)

later
he would sit in the shade, resting his eyes
from all this foreign light, the ache
of the ceiling sky,
and read some improving *fabliau* of far-off urban manners,
about Walter Mosley's Socrates, perhaps, a character
of heartening inscape and outwit: something
dry, acerbic, some other takes on gravity, misdemeanour
and what's real.

        After all, when the great hero
        returned home at last, a decade
        gone, the dog too
                   had his day.

15

Meanwhile, in that classical *interim* between
breakfast and mid-day, between
entering and coming, between just now
and now
he stretches out his bare arms
in a brief semaphore of something
like *tant pis!* and returns the stare
of the buzzard up in his favourite fir-tree.

Now look at it another way.
From his perch a hundred feet away
the bird can see the pale branches of arms and legs,
like a disconsolate arrangement
of finical kindling, not at all relaxed,
not preening after breakfast,
the eyes open and staring into days.

Afterwards

1

Geography Lesson

So what's the point? he keeps asking.

The one that's furthest south, furthest away
from little England, from the northern regulations of the day,
the chasing past; it's the away-ness
he's after, 'the furthest south you can go
on dry land'...

but this one resting on its sharpened tip
as on a lie, a false Hope indeed
so close to False Bay, is not what he is after:
the truth is a little to the east
and more unexciting – Cape Agulhas
with its huddle of dismal rocks
bruises but does not stun.

Proof lies in the map-book, but Hope
still rides its high prow out into the bluer sea.
This false and lovely notion is
(so it seems to him) as true as ever.
Here two oceans, Atlantic and Indian, the cool and the warm,
are pouring together, confusing all the time,
and maybe that's the trouble.

2

Same Place, Different Time

The spectator sits in the car, window down,
holding on to his pathetic fallacies, and stares out southwards
over the cold steel waves, all the unbearable beauties
of the Cape behind him, unable to bind

the long ribbons of the past firmly to himself,
or let them, finally, go –
those ribbons that run away from him like roads across landscapes,
anywhere from Worcester and Malmesbury
to Port Elizabeth and East London
or the criss-cross tangles round Cape Town.

Right here, there are two oceans in collusion
about direction, wind, temperature, even fish...
right here where the southern right whales
are closing in to mate along the shores
now that July's running into August.
Spring must be coming in on the tides.

They roll around in the harbour at Hermanus,
lolling for themselves alone, two or three scouts
or early birds ahead of the pod, a scene so
emotionally perfect that it forces the spectator's mind

to stray again... for whom or what are they 'right',
these giants of frolic, glossy with water as one
bursts the surface for a second or two and launches off
a spume into the air?
They have every right – they *are* right – to be here, but
as usual the truth lies elsewhere:
these were the creatures we once believed we had the 'right'
to seize and flay for their virtues of oil and flesh.
(Yes, it's *'the light from plundered tallow'* again.)

Self-awards and rewards beyond need
are a special trick we're bloody good at.
The spectator tries to gaze beyond
the sly horizon's curve. *Is it a kind of corner?*
he used to wonder when he was first taken to a beach –

Whitley Bay next to Tynemouth, if I remember, where
the old Morris 8 drove down to the (for once) bright blue water
and his mother pointed to the Spanish City, that louche alhambra
of simple pleasures, dreamed up by her father
when that other century was just starting its fun and games...

Now as it's finishing, he watches under the sun the choppy white horses
flicker over the sea like bubbles frothing
across a crater dark as pinotage. *Well, honestly!*
(OK, look it up – 'krater'!)

He switches on and drives away
westwards towards the Cape of Good Hope.
Then he turns north again.

3

View from the Saloon

Not to be permitted, then, any kind
of harmony. So now,
even much later, he can see when he
closes his eyes, through the red-lid mist,
some of the distances and other seasons of the past,
what they have kept bright for him.

He can see from his comfortable saloon
the black beetle cars flash to and fro past the airport,
and droning long-haul wagons that no one's going to
draw round into a *laager*, and the formal 'informal settlements'
where refugees from District Six went after the bulldozers
rebuilt their lives on shifting sands –

it comes right up to the edge of the N2,
this cardboard city with its tarpaulin terraces
and bin-bag boulevards, and here when it rains
for days these driftwood homes drift apart
on sloping ground, less resilient than
the torn swatches of white plastic streaming out
from the highway fences, all waving in the same direction.

The visitor, the observer, the spectator
fingers his minute attentions and tests the absorbing self
he struggles with, struggles to turn outwards back
into the world, especially in a land where once we all

took a terrible funny turn out of wildness.
He has been up and down this route many times.
One day, undistracted by the mountain under
its table-cloth, he sees ahead a man and a boy
driving a dozen cows and a goat or two – now as he passes
beneath them they are overhead, crossing
a glassed-in walkway over the traffic tide,
everyday Africans about their business, eager to get
to the other side. The spectator believes
it is not sentimental eyewash to admire
their purposes, as he brakes, changes down
and pulls in behind a black family in their white Mercedes.

4

Elsewhere's View from the Saloon

He stops by the roadside in that spooky countryside
round this other Elim, keeping his usual eye on birds.

Or was it nearer Heidelberg, or Albertinia? It was near some dusty *dorp*
where it goes very quiet in the afternoons,
the sort of place where you might be invited
through to the back of the house and in a shed
an old lady might show you on the wall the picture of her father
in 1930s grey shirt, friend of Louis Weichardt, and the flags
pinned up in the corner, moth-holes in the black, red and white designs
copied from the old country… Still a few weeds
from the *broederbond* in poor soil where there's a dearth of
springs and palm trees, a lack of tamarisks.

At the end of a brown field he sees them dancing,
frolicking and flapping, keeping their distance;
at least they look more like kids enjoying themselves
than politicians pretending to be serious.
More than the sugarbird or the hornbill or
the high mewling sea eagle, these blue cranes
with their long pipes of neck and their skittering stalky legs
and their pale caps carry a terrible weight that means
nothing to them and everything to us.

No twitcher, more of a spectator. But he knows
they carry fifty million years of the planet, these birds,
and this is their region – this one of the fifteen tribes.
It does not really matter whether he survives or
for how long, and although for that moment
there was nothing more important than
his sight of them in the sunlight, and what
might linger in his memory for a while,

what matters, he knows, is that they
should survive, these birds with their foreign necks
and the grey-blue north-south dazzle of their feathers.

They are no invention, however much their display
is like the decor of a pretty room.
You can't imagine, the excitement of such grey regalia.

Seeing them is a kind of signature
of trust in *res publica*,
                         as if he might say
(and he smiles at his pretentious self)
Civis Africanus sum,

though they have no good reason
to trust him, he tells himself,
motoring away from the strange brown fields near Elim.

Coda

or, *The Tail of the Tale*

Mapping his passion.
He is intent for the hundredth time
over the map of this place
that has come so strangely into his life,
trying to translate the story of this western cape
and the continent of origins before the time of words.

And it comes to him suddenly – it is the name
of Good Hope
pulling him hardest, even more
than the edgy precarious land
stopping before the sea,

and what is it that is sparking up his synapses?
Words again, he realises, as much as the place itself,
the naming of names (else how to tell?) –

a much smaller drop of blue than this,
merely a moment compared to a lifetime,
    north-west of the city where he grew up,

              a lough in Northumberland called Sweethope.

Memory, generous for once, lets him see it again
for the first time,
            the early sun behind him on a June morning,
glimpsing it from a distance, water-colour through trees –

some blue eye and hope's lovely lashes.
Some sweet hope.

Notes

'*Veronica Lake*': The 1940s Hollywood actor Veronica Lake, she of the peekaboo hairstyle, was born Constance Ockelman. *The Blue Dahlia* is among her better-known films. St Veronica's handkerchief is alleged to have shown the face of Christ after she wiped his face on the way to Calvary.

'*Bridling at Birdsong*': *The Bird Symphony* by the Finnish Sami poet, musician, artist and film-maker Nils-Aslak Valkeapää, recorded on site in the nature reserve of Sapmi, was awarded special prize for music in the *Prix Italia* for Radio in Rome in 1993.

'*Our Friends in the North*': the title of an award-winning BBC television serial written by Peter Flannery, shown in 1996, and thought by many to be one of the finest political TV dramas ever made.
'*The spuggies are fledged*' is the epigraph to Basil Bunting's *Briggflatts*.

'*Just So Long (As)*': Umhlanga Rocks is a town on the KwaZulu-Natal coast, now a northern suburb of Greater Durban. Pronunciation is, very approximately, *Oomshlongger*.
'wolves': there are of course no wolves in South Africa – Rider Haggard was referring to jackals.

'*No End of a Lesson*': Kipling's poem was first published in *The Times* of 29 July 1901, during the Boer War, in which Afrikaners gave Britain its biggest military shock since the Indian Mutiny.
'Irene' has three syllables here, following the Greek.

'*The Peppered Moth*': 'aftermath' originally meant a 'second mowing' in a single season.
Much of the work of the German artist Anselm Kiefer (b. 1945) explores the dark side of Germany's past, some of it influenced by the poetry of Paul Celan. The German for beech forest is, of course, Buchenwald, the name given to the concentration camp near Weimar. It was opened in 1937, and by 1945 some 56,000 people had died there. The Nazis wanted a 'neutral' name, one that could not, for example, be associated with Goethe.

The German-Jewish poet Heinrich Heine (1797–1856) famously wrote in 1821 (exactly one hundred years before Hitler became Führer of the

Nazi Party): 'Where they burn books, they will, in the end, burn human beings too.' On 10 May 1933 bonfires were lit in German cities in which proscribed books by both Jewish and non-Jewish writers were publicly burnt by Nazi students and Stormtroopers.

For information used in this poem I am indebted to Simon Schama, *Landscape and Memory* (1995).

'*Pepper's Ghost*': John Henry Pepper first showed in the 1880s the technique of theatrical illusion which later bore his name: lighting, mirrors and plate glass provided an on-stage ghost.

'*Mountainwood*': Helshoogte is a mountain pass near Stellenbosch; Languedoc is in the same winelands area of the Western Cape.
7: Boerland: 'boer' is 'farmer' in Afrikaans.
12: '*braii*' is Afrikaans for 'barbecue'.

'*Afterwards*'
1 'Geography Lesson': Cape Agulhas is a point on the coast further south than the Cape of Good Hope.
3 'View from the Saloon': District Six was a cosmopolitan residential area of Cape Town whose mostly non-white inhabitants were forcibly removed by the apartheid government in the 1970s, and the houses bulldozed.
4 'Elsewhere's View from the Saloon': Elim by origin was an oasis near the Red Sea where the Israelites camped after leaving Egypt.
dorp is Afrikaans for 'town' (cf. English 'thorpe').
Louis Weichardt was founder of a South African nationalist right-wing group called 'Greyshirts' in the 1930s, taking the Nazi Brownshirts as their model. The *Broederbond* (Brotherhood) was an Afrikaner fascist society which played a major role in the last century in the establishment and maintenance of the apartheid government.